The Development of Western Civilization

*Narrative Essays in the History of Our Tradition from
Its Origins in Ancient Israel and Greece to the Present*

Edited by Edward W. Fox

*Professor of Modern European History
Cornell University*

THE AGE OF REFORMATION

By E. HARRIS HARBISON

W9-AKY-954

The Age of Reformation

E. HARRIS HARBISON

*

Cornell University Press

ITHACA AND LONDON

Copyright 1955 by Cornell University

All rights reserved. Except for brief quotations in a review, this book, or parts thereof, must not be reproduced in any form without permission in writing from the publisher. For information address Cornell University Press, 124 Roberts Place, Ithaca, New York 14850.

First published 1955 by Cornell University Press
Published in the United Kingdom by Cornell University Press Ltd.
2-4 Brook Street, London W1Y 1AA
Sixteenth printing 1973

International Standard Book Number 0-8014-9844-9

PRINTED IN THE UNITED STATES OF AMERICA
BY VAIL BALLOU PRESS, INC., BINGHAMTON, NEW YORK

Foreword

THE proposition that each generation must rewrite history is more widely quoted than practiced. In the field of college texts on western civilization, the conventional accounts have been revised, and sources and supplementary materials have been developed; but it is too long a time since the basic narrative has been rewritten to meet the rapidly changing needs of new college generations. In the mid-twentieth century such an account must be brief, well written, and based on unquestioned scholarship and must assume almost no previous historical knowledge on the part of the reader. It must provide a coherent analysis of the development of western civilization and its basic values. It must, in short, constitute a systematic introduction to the collective memory of that tradition which we are being asked to defend. This series of narrative essays was undertaken in an effort to provide such a text for an introductory history survey course and is being published in the present form in the belief that the requirements of that one course reflected a need that is coming to be widely recognized.

Now that the classic languages, the Bible, the great historical novels, even most non-American history, have dropped out of the normal college preparatory program, it is imperative that a text in the history of European civilization be fully self-explanatory. This means not only that it must begin at the beginning, with the origins of our civilization in ancient Israel and Greece, but that it must introduce every name or event that takes an integral place in the account and ruthlessly delete all others no matter how firmly imbedded in historical protocol. Only thus simplified and complete will the narrative present a sufficiently clear outline of those major trends and developments that have led from the beginning of our recorded time to the most pressing of our current problems. This simplification, however, need not involve intellectual dilution or evasion. On the contrary, it can effectively raise rather than lower the level of presentation. It is on this assumption that the present series has been based, and each contributor has been urged to write for a mature and literate audience. It is hoped, therefore, that the essays may also prove profitable and rewarding to readers outside the college classroom.

The plan of the first part of the series is to sketch, in related essays, the narrative of our history from its origins to the eve of the French Revolution; each is to be written by a recognized scholar and is designed to serve as the basic reading for one week in a semester course. The developments of the nineteenth and twentieth centuries will be covered in a succeeding series which will provide the same quantity of reading material for each week of the second semester. This scale of presentation has been adopted in the conviction that any understanding of the central problem of the preservation of the integrity and dignity of the individual human being depends first on an examination of the origins of our tradition in the politics and philosophy of the ancient Greeks and the religion of the ancient Hebrews and then on a relatively more detailed knowledge of its recent development within our industrial urban society.

The decision to devote equal space to twenty-five centuries and to a century and a half was based on analogy with the human memory. Those events most remote tend to be remembered in least detail but often with a sense of clarity and perspective that is absent in more recent and more crowded recollections. If the roots of our tradition must be identified, their relation to the present must be carefully developed. The nearer the narrative approaches contemporary times, the more difficult and complicated this becomes. Recent experience must be worked over more carefully and in more detail if it is to contribute effectively to an understanding of the contemporary world.

It may be objected that the series attempts too much. The attempt is being made, however, on the assumption that any historical development should be susceptible of meaningful treatment on any scale and in the realization that a very large proportion of today's college students do not have more time to invest in this part of their education. The practical alternative appears to lie between some attempt to create a new brief account of the history of our tradition and the abandonment of any serious effort to communicate the essence of that tradition to all but a handful of our students. It is the conviction of everyone contributing to this series that the second alternative must not be accepted by default.

In a series covering such a vast sweep of time, few scholars would find themselves thoroughly at home in the fields covered by more than one or two of the essays. This means, in practice, that almost every essay should be written by a different author. In spite of apparent drawbacks, this procedure promises real advantages. Each contributor will be in a position to set higher standards of accuracy and insight in an essay encompassing a major portion of the field of his life's work than could ordinarily be expected in surveys of some ten or twenty centuries. The inevitable discontinuity of style and interpretation could be modified by editorial co-ordination; but it was felt that some discontinuity was in itself desirable. No illusion is more easily acquired by the student in an elementary course, or is more prejudicial to the efficacy of such a course, than that a single smoothly articulated text represents the very substance of history itself. If the shift from author to author, week by week, raises difficulties for the beginning student, they are difficulties that will not so much impede his progress as contribute to his growth.

In this essay, *The Age of Reformation*, Mr. E. Harris Harbison has at once described the crisis of faith and conscience which wracked western Europe at the beginning of our modern era and set it firmly in the context of the political and social struggle which constitutes the history of the sixteenth century. That some of our deepest and most divisive problems today stem from this period of religious revolution has long been recognized, and various aspects of the subject have been searched and analyzed with a thoroughness commensurate with their significance. There have, however, been surprisingly few synthetic studies of the period as a whole. The Reformation, the religious drama of the rending of the single church of Christendom into rival sects, has become a field of history in itself. More than any other single period in the development of our society, the Reformation has placed the ultimate responsibility not only for moral and social but also religious decisions within the conscience of the individual, and so it has produced an entire literature of biography. This same period has been taken as the test case of modern sociological history in its effort to demonstrate that ideals and guiding principles are not fully understandable apart from the men who held them nor the men wholly comprehensible as individuals divorced from the society in which they lived. It is, therefore, of utmost importance that an introduction to this period should deal not with one or another of its dramatic and fateful aspects, but that it should trace, in a single brief pattern, as Mr. Harbison does, the outlines, interlocked and interwoven as they were, of the various phases that constituted the totality of what he calls the "Age of Reformation."

The author and the editor wish to express their gratitude to Mr. Garrett Mattingly and Mr. Maurice D. Lee, Jr., for many helpful suggestions.

EDWARD WHITING FOX

Ithaca, New York
November, 1954

Contents

THE AGE OF REFORMATION

Introduction

THE sixteenth century was an Age of Reformation. In the first place, this means that the century witnessed the Protestant Reformation, that revolt from the Roman Catholic Church led by Martin Luther and others which ended the ecclesiastical unity of western Christendom. This is the common usage of the term, and it was in this sense that Preserved Smith used it a generation ago when he entitled his masterly interpretation of the period, *The Age of the Reformation*. But there was the Catholic Reformation as well, a movement which the great German historian, Leopold von Ranke, called "the Counter Reformation." If one considers the whole religious side of the picture, the century should properly be called "the Age of the Reformations." Recently there has been a tendency to broaden the concept still further. Gerhard Ritter calls his recent fine synthesis *The Reorganization of Europe in the Sixteenth Century: Ecclesiastical and Political Change in the Age of the Reformation and the Religious Wars*. "Reformation" here is part of a wider "Reorganization" of economic, political, and religious life which characterized the century. In the present essay the word "Reformation" will be used in its ordinary reference to the reform, both Protestant and Catholic, of religious practices and beliefs. But the title is meant to suggest a broader theme: the readjustment and reorganization of ideas and institutions at every level which marked the period between the appearance of Luther (1517) and the deaths of Philip II of Spain (1598) and Elizabeth of England (1603).

The danger is oversimplification. Our minds demand order and sequence, rationality and intelligibility, in the accounts that we give of the past. The briefer the account, the more deceptive is the order that we must necessarily impose on the material if the result is to make sense. The sixteenth century cannot be reduced to a formula. The truth escapes us not because we do not know enough facts, but because the relationships of the facts are so complicated. What the present account tries to do is to ask the most significant questions, to suggest answers upon which recent scholarship is generally agreed, to point to the wide areas in which we know either too little or too much to be clear and precise about any answer, and to hint at the frame of mind in which any answers to historical problems should be formulated. The best description of this frame of mind is comprehensiveness. Comprehensiveness in research and understanding must always be the historian's first rule. He cannot afford to be blind to any of the various factors—economic, social, political, intellectual, or religious—which enter into any given historical situation. If from what follows the reader gains some sense of the complex interplay of all these factors in the history of the sixteenth century, the purpose of the essay will have been fulfilled.

CHAPTER I

The European World about 1500

Human Geography

AT THE ancient city of Basel the river Rhine, flowing westward from Lake Constance, turns northward to begin its course through Germany to the North Sea. It was here that one of the two great church councils of the fifteenth century had been held. Here one of the famous universities of Europe was located; here John Froben, one of the great printers of the sixteenth century, had his shop; and here Erasmus, the prince of Humanists, spent his later years. Basel was a center of trade and of industry as well as of scholarship and religion. It experienced something of all the major movements of the century: the development of capitalism, Humanism, and Protestant reform.

There is a sense in which this small, busy city could be called the center of sixteenth-century Europe. If one should take a map of the continent, place the point of a compass on Basel, and describe a circle with a radius of five hundred miles, this circle would include the civilized heart of Europe in the Age of the Reformation. Within it were most of France and Germany, the southeastern corner of England and the northeastern corner of Spain, the Netherlands, Switzerland, and northern Italy. Outside it were most of the British Isles, all of Scandinavia, Poland, Russia, Hungary and the Balkans, southern Italy, and most of the Iberian peninsula. Generally speaking, both density of population and accumulation of wealth were greater within this imaginary circle than outside it.

The largest concentrations of population and accumulations of wealth—buildings and industries, ships, agricultural surpluses, and goods of all kinds—were in northern Italy, eastern France, the Rhine valley, and the Netherlands. There were probably over ten times as many inhabitants per square mile in these regions as there were in Russia, Scandinavia, or Scotland. England, Spain, eastern Germany, and the Balkans would fall somewhere in between. In the latter part of the century, England's four million inhabitants were only half Spain's eight million, and these in turn were but half France's sixteen (the figures are, of course, very rough). The German-speaking states contained perhaps fifteen to twenty million, Italy perhaps twelve. The contrast of population concentration within and without the circle is most evident in the fact that the vast area of Poland and Lithuania probably had very few more inhabitants than the Netherlands (three million or less).

Beyond the circle to the east the shores of the Mediterranean were still relatively thickly settled, as they had been since Roman times. Constantinople was one of the largest cities in Europe. There was still a "Mediterranean World," bound together by the trackless highway formed by the inland sea. But this sea was dominated until late in the century by an Asiatic and non-Christian people, the Ottoman Turks, and so there was a spiritual as well as a material reason for saying that the circle round Basel included the core of Christian Europe. It is not far wrong to say that the

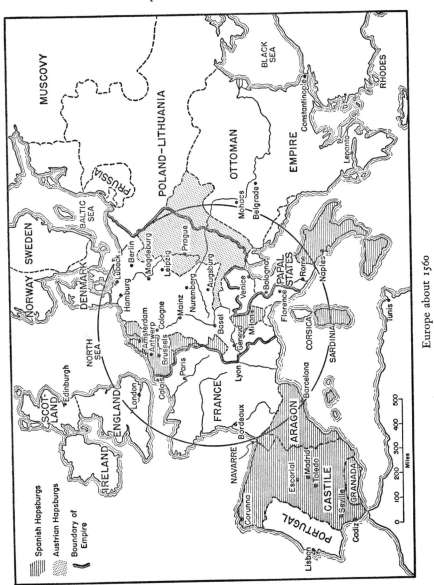

Europe about 1560

MUSCOVY

BLACK
SEA

RHODES

POLAND–LITHUANIA

OTTOMAN

EMPIRE

Constantinople

Lepanto

NORWAY SWEDEN

DENMARK

BALTIC
SEA

PRUSSIA

Berlin

Magdeburg

Prague

Leipzig

Lübeck

Mohacs

Belgrade

Hamburg

Mainz

Nuremberg

Augsburg

PAPAL
STATES

Bologna

Rome

Naples

Amsterdam

Antwerp

Cologne

Basel

Venice

Florence

Brussels

Milan

Geneva

NORTH
SEA

Paris

Lyon

CORSICA

SARDINIA

Tunis

Edinburgh

SCOT-
LAND

London

Calais

FRANCE

Bordeaux

Barcelona

ARAGON

IRELAND

ENGLAND

NAVARRE

Escorial

Madrid

Toledo

CASTILE

GRANADA

Sevilla

Cadiz

PORTUGAL

Corunna

Lisbon

Miles

0   100   200   300   400   500

Spanish Hapsburgs

Austrian Hapsburgs

Boundary of
Empire

Ottoman Empire, Russia, the Scandinavian countries, and even England and Spain, were peripheral or "frontier" regions, relatively far removed in either a material or spiritual way from the center of Christendom. At any rate, cultivated persons living within the five-hundred-mile circle about Basel were aware that at any point beyond its circumference one might run into border regions (as in Wales or Scotland), trackless uncivilized areas (as in northeastern Europe), or actual frontiers of Christendom (like the boundaries between Christians and Moslems in Hungary). It is no coincidence that this book is concerned almost exclusively with events which took place within this circle—with the significant exceptions of Spain and England, peripheral lands which played leading roles in sixteenth-century Europe.

In terms of human geography, Europe was much larger than it is today. If Erasmus in Basel were writing to a friend in Madrid, he would have to count upon his letter taking anywhere from one to three months to reach its destination. Official dispatches from London to Paris might get through in two days with exceptional luck, but they would usually take a week and might take over a month. Crossing the Mediterranean from north to south was generally a matter of one or two weeks; from west to east, a matter of one or two months. The fastest travel was by sea. On the Mediterranean oar-propelled galleys with favorable winds made record times of 125 miles per day. The heavier galleons, built for the Atlantic and relying exclusively on sails, would not do so well. On land the fastest postal organizations would sometimes cover eighty-five miles a day. News of the battle of Lepanto in 1571 took eleven days to get from the Gulf of Corinth to Venice, and another thirteen days to reach Paris and Madrid. A year later news of the

1572

Massacre of St. Bartholomew's Eve took fourteen days to get from Paris to Madrid. As Fernand Braudel puts it, the European world still had Roman dimensions. In terms of ease and speed of communications, Europe in the sixteenth century was larger than the whole world today.

In a study of the economic, social, and political organization of sixteenth-century Europe, this matter of scale must constantly be borne in mind. A city like Basel could not exist without the plodding mule trains and clumsy river boats which linked it with other cities, with the countryside, and with the sea. Venice had long been dependent upon her Mediterranean sea routes; Bristol, Lisbon, and Cadiz soon became dependent upon their ties to America and Asia. But the struggle against time and distance was never easy. Mule trains could be robbed or diverted hundreds of miles by war. Fleets could be delayed for months or destroyed altogether by storms. Whether it was a Venetian merchant awaiting the Flanders fleet, or the king of Spain anxiously expecting word from his governor in the Netherlands, or Calvin hoping for good news from Scotland, merchandise and news traveled with baffling slowness. Life was still more local and provincial than it is easy to imagine in the twentieth century. There were strict limits imposed by the technology of communications upon how large a business could be developed, how extensive an empire could be held together, or how strictly a movement like the Protestant Reformation could be controlled by any single leader.

Social Classes

Europe was still overwhelmingly rural. Nine out of ten persons made their living directly from the soil, from agriculture or some closely related pursuit. The tenth might be an artisan, a merchant, a lawyer, or a royal official, who lived in a city or town and bought his food and clothing with money which represented the profit from his business or the salary of his profession. Most of the urban centers were small by modern standards. Wittenberg, where Luther began his career as reformer, was a little town of about 2,000, typical of the vast majority of European towns. Geneva, a large city for its day, had 16,000 inhabitants when Calvin arrived there in 1536. Probably only a half-dozen cities in Europe exceeded 100,000 in population, among them Venice, Florence, Paris, and London, which grew from 75,000 inhabitants in 1500 to 200,000 by 1600.

In spite of their small number, however, the town-dwellers or *bourgeoisie* were the dynamic element in European society. The three traditional classes of mediaeval society—nobility, clergy, and peasantry—were still the only classes recognized in much of law and literature. But the class-in-between, the "middle class" as it came to be called years later, was the class which was actually building the foundations of a new Europe.

It is impossible to describe these "classes" briefly and simply and still with accuracy. Each had a characteristic general function in society, but there were great differences of rank within each and the lines of separation were not always clear. Further, as the century progressed, there was increasing social mobility—probably more than there had been since Roman times, though small by modern American standards. Men could and did move up or down the social ladder in increasing numbers.

The nobles had lost much of their military power throughout Europe, but their social prestige was almost untouched and their political influence was still far beyond that of the rising middle class. There was enormous difference, however, between a great duke with lands and power a king might envy, and an impoverished baron caught in the squeeze between rising prices and a small fixed income. In some countries, as in England and Castile, the nobility shaded off at its base into a rural middle class of gentry, whose titles were not hereditary but who were definitely something more than yeomen or free farmers.

The clergy were a class in the sense that they possessed recognized privileges and immunities as a result of their ordination. Unlike the nobility, they were part of a European-wide organization, subject in theory at least to a centralized discipline. But as in the case of the nobles there was a vast difference between a wealthy bishop or abbot and a humble parish priest or mendicant friar. And at the base of the hierarchy it was sometimes difficult in practice to draw the line between those in minor orders and laymen, since almost anyone who could read Latin (like university students) was presumed to be of the clergy no matter how secular his manner of living might be.

The peasants were no more uniform than the nobles and clergy, unless it was in the common obligation to long, hard manual labor. There were complex differences in legal and economic status between different sorts of peasants—free, unfree, and semifree—in different parts of Europe. Generally speaking, they were somewhat more free and better off in western than in eastern Europe. But everywhere their lot was hard.

Between long hours of labor, and nights spent on straw with a good round log for a pillow; under the shadow of death and, worse still, of sickness unrelieved by anything but the crudest medical science; in great discomfort and many fears; in the midst of beauty untouched by any ugliness save that of dirt, disease, or death, the common people passed their lives.[1]

Of all the classes, the most difficult to describe is the middle class. Some scholars would narrow it by definition to include only the bourgeoisie or townsmen and to exclude the country gentry. A wealthy banker with interests in a dozen different cities, a Roman lawyer serving as crown official, a manager of a silver mine, a ship captain, a master of a mediaeval craft gild, a journeyman worker—each of these was, strictly speaking, a bourgeois. But there might be very little in common between them, except that they were neither nobles, nor clergy, nor peasants. At the top of the bourgeoisie wealthy merchants were continually acquiring land, buying titles, and becoming nobles. At the bottom journeymen and apprentices constituted a small but growing industrial proletariat in some towns. In between there were "the butcher, the baker, the candlestick maker," the small bourgeoisie, members of long-established craft gilds. Obviously it is confusing to include all such persons under any single label like "bourgeoisie," even though historians are sometimes compelled to do so in order to emphasize the fact that they all depended upon the town for their livelihood and cannot be included in the three classes of mediaeval society.

Let us say simply that the bourgeois was the man who made the busy towns and cities of Europe what they were. Most typically he was a man on the move and on the make, building or expanding a business, acting as agent for a noble or a king, serving as notary or legal agent, teaching privately or publicly. All these activities were potentially subversive of the established order, an order which still thought in

[1] H. F. M. Prescott, *Mary Tudor* (New York, 1953), p. 12. Quoted by permission of The Macmillan Company.

terms of feudal obligations, traditional rights, and custom. The curiosity of explorers and the desire for gain of merchant princes were dangerous to the *status quo*. For instance, many a feudal landowner was directly affected by Columbus' discovery of America when the influx of gold and silver from the New World led to a spectacular increase in prices, since inflation hurt everyone who lived on a relatively fixed income as did the nobility. The work of Roman lawyers, hired by kings to investigate feudal privileges, was as dangerous to the nobility as the criticism of Humanist scholars was to the clergy. This is not to say that the explorers and merchants, the lawyers and scholars, were consciously revolutionary. The vast majority of them were not. But the capitalistic enterprises, the absolute monarchies, and the new ideas which they were developing were to prove infinitely destructive of mediaeval institutions and conceptions. This is what we mean when we say that the towns and the townsmen were the dynamic element in European society.

Economic Revolution and Social Change

In the early sixteenth century the European economy was expanding with unprecedented rapidity. The mule trains which traveled the roads and the ships which sailed the seas carried more freight and cargo every year. Old industries like clothmaking flourished and new industries like printing, cannon founding, and the production of silk offered novel opportunities for employment and profit. The Portuguese rounded the Cape of Good Hope just before the century began and thus short-circuited the ancient overland trade route from the Levant to India. Thus a cheaper, faster way was found of transporting the spices and textiles of the East to a Europe avid for such luxuries. Columbus' discovery of a New World across the Atlantic eventually opened up a vast new hinterland to the European economy.

It is often pointed out that as a result of the great discoveries of the fifteenth century there was a significant shift of the economic center of gravity from the Mediterranean city-states to the nations bordering on the Atlantic. This is both true and important, but we are learning that Venice did not necessarily decline as Portugal and Spain rose in the early sixteenth century. Nor did Portugal and Spain immediately fade out of the picture as England, France, and the Netherlands began to build up their trade with America and Asia toward the end of the sixteenth century. We are dealing here with absolute additions to the total commerce of Europe, and although a competitive element was certainly involved, the relative decline of commerce in one area or another is not so striking as the great increase in European trade as a whole.

Economic history knows no sharp breaks, but the acceleration of economic development at the close of the fifteenth and beginning of the sixteenth century is so striking that a great French scholar, Henri Hauser, insists that it can only be described as an economic revolution. Here, he says, is the beginning of the modern economic world: capitalistic practices applied widely to finance and commerce, more narrowly to industry and agriculture; an expanding, competitive economy, now first beginning to show signs in some areas of the familiar business cycle of boom and bust; the earliest appearance of something like international money markets (at Antwerp, Lyons, and Genoa), the first mechanized industry turning out a standardized product and using the principle of interchangeable parts (printing by moveable type), and an urban proletariat using the weapon of the strike (at Lyons in 1539). The main features of nineteenth-century European economy are certainly present in embryo by 1550.

The most important fact about sixteenth-century European society is that it was a society undergoing rapid change, change which few if any understood.

The pace was more rapid than anything Europe had known for centuries. As trade and industry expanded, prices rose, slowly at first, then precipitously. The opportunities for amassing a fortune multiplied. Individuals, families, and even whole towns rose from poverty to wealth in what seemed very brief spans of time. At the same time others saw themselves forced off their land by grasping landlords or bankrupted overnight by "monopolists" and "usurers." The common man had no way of understanding such things, except as the works of God or the Devil. There were no secular rationalizations through which Europeans could understand economic and social change. Certainly there was no trace of the twentieth-century American assumption that change is natural and good. In the brilliant analysis of the ills of society in the first book of Sir Thomas More's *Utopia* (1516), recent change is generally condemned and attributed to the two classic Christian sins, pride and greed. In Utopia, the author's imaginary society, time passes but there is no essential change. The more deeply we study sixteenth-century literature, the more fundamental we find the sense of changeless social pattern to be. God created the world and man; there is a "great chain of being" in which each creature has his appointed place and function; any disturbance of this order of existence stems from sin and leads to anarchy. These in general were the assumptions of Christian Europe. They hardly provided any but the most naïve explanations of the "sturdy beggars" who wandered helplessly about England in Elizabeth's reign (we would call them "unemployed"), or the peasants on the continent who were moving off the land to better their condition, perhaps by becoming miners like Luther's father, or the wealthy bankers who sometimes seemed to have more real power than earls or dukes. Unfamiliar and disturbing things were happening every day, with no apparent explanation and no moral or religious justification. The only categories through which contemporaries of Luther could understand the impact of what we call capitalism upon their society were pride and greed.

The economic and social forces were building up for revolutionary change about 1500. But since men are ultimately free and not the puppets of such forces, the direction which such change would take could not be guessed in advance.

The European States

Political change was developing in 1500 almost as rapidly as economic and social change. At certain points, political developments were shaped and even determined by the economic forces we have described; at others, the changes in political institutions and boundaries shaped or determined the economic developments. At all points, the two kinds of change were closely related, as even statesmen of the time were vaguely aware.

Europe in the sixteenth century was composed of independent "states," separated by fairly definite boundaries, controlled by central governments headed usually by kings or princes, competing with each other for power and prestige in peace and war. However modern these features

Feudal =

might seem, the political institutions of these states, as well
as their relations with each other, showed unmistakable links
with the mediaeval past. Governments were neither so su-
premely "sovereign" over all the territories within their
boundaries nor so admittedly "sovereign" with respect to
other governments as those of three or four centuries later.
A sixteenth-century monarch had far more independence of
action and actual power over his territories than his mediaeval predecessors, but he could not hold a candle to a
modern totalitarian dictator in the irresponsibility and efficiency of his power.

Generally speaking, the rulers of Europe about 1500 were
stronger than they had been a century earlier. In Spain,
France, and England the civil wars of the fifteenth century
had decimated the feudal nobility, exasperated the middle
classes, and made the lot of the peasants more miserable.
Wherever a monarch of any force of character at all appeared, he found he had the solid backing of the bourgeoisie,
who much preferred royal tyranny to feudal anarchy since
it meant the establishment of law and order over wider areas
of the land. A ruler who was serious about putting down
overmighty subjects could usually count upon the financial
support of the middle classes. Money could buy the services
of Roman lawyers, who were adept at investigating feudal
rights and expanding the area of royal jurisdiction. Money
could also buy artillery, which was too expensive for most
nobles and which could pulverize feudal castles if need be.
A king or prince who could tap the new sources of wealth
was in a position to rest his power not upon the older idea
of feudal "suzerainty" over individual vassals, but upon the
more modern idea of "sovereignty" over all "subjects"
within certain territorial boundaries, whether they were

Suzerainty

nobles, priests, peasants, or townsmen. The idea of sovereignty was not clearly defined till 1576, by Jean Bodin, but it was no accident that the political thought of the early sixteenth century concentrated upon the dual theme of the rights of rulers and the duties of subjects. The trend was toward strong, centralized government. In theory as in practice the need of the age was for authority rather than for liberty, for order first and freedom afterward.

The Western Monarchies: France, Spain, and England

France was the political hub of sixteenth-century Europe. Although its eastern frontier was not so far east as it is today, the kingdom of France was the largest territory in Europe under a single, effective government. There was a growing sense of French nationality which was paralleled by the growing power of the royal government in Paris. There were still great duchies like Britanny which were relatively independent even though united to the crown, great families like that of Bourbon which controlled large holdings of land and could act much as they pleased, and institutions like the Estates-General, the provincial estates, and the *parlements* (or high courts) which could hamper the royal will on occasions. But nowhere else in Europe was there such a large and relatively homogeneous people under a single government which could make its will felt in all corners of the land. As Niccolo Machiavelli contemplated France in 1513 from an Italy which was a welter of independent city-states, he was filled with a mixture of admiration and envy. When he thought of the problem of successfully unifying large territories, the two contemporary examples which sprang first to his mind were the despotism shorn =

of the Ottoman Empire and the more constitutional monarchy of France.

In the early part of the century France was the aggressive
and disturbing element in European international affairs.
It was tempting for the French king to divert the energies
of great nobles who had recently been shorn of much of
their power at home to military adventures abroad, and
generally the nobles welcomed the chance to find fame and
plunder in a foreign war. After the middle of the century,
as we shall see, the French found themselves in the throes
of a civil war so devastating and crippling to the royal power
that all the gains of the past three centuries seemed to have
been lost. But until 1560 France appeared to be the strongest
and most aggressive power on the continent.

Strictly speaking, there was as yet no "Spain" in 1500.
The Iberian peninsula was divided among Portugal in the
west, Castile in the center, and Aragon (whose king was
also king of Catalonia and Valencia) in the east. Ferdinand
of Aragon was husband to Isabella of Castile, and this meant
unity of the two eastern realms in foreign policy. To speak
of "Spain" had meaning, therefore, outside the peninsula.
But except for the famous Inquisition, there was no institution common to the two kingdoms. Each had its own councils
and courts and representative assemblies, and a customs
barrier ran between them. Within each kingdom, however,
the same sort of expansion of the royal power at the expense
of feudal nobles and local rights was taking place as had
taken place somewhat earlier in France. Backed by the
towns and their representatives, both Ferdinand of Aragon
and Isabella of Castile clipped the wings of their unruly
nobility, centralized administration in royal councils, and
increased the revenues of the crown. The growing Portu-

guese empire in the East and the newly founded Castilian empire in the New World were great potential sources of economic strength which were to be realized as the century progressed.

The peculiar problem of the Iberian peninsula was that there were three religions existing in uneasy balance: the Christian, the Moslem, and the Jewish. During the Dark Ages, Spain had been the most tolerant and enlightened land in Europe, but the long crusade of Christians against Moslems culminating in 1492 in the conquest of Granada, the last Moslem foothold on the peninsula, gradually exacerbated Christian feelings. By the close of the fifteenth century Christian Spain was becoming the most intolerant nation in Europe. The narrow piety of Queen Isabella had much to do with the change. But hatred and jealousy of the mercantile success of the Jews and the agricultural ability of the Moors were widespread among the middle classes and even among the nobility, and the new policy of persecuting all those not of "pure blood"—meaning Christian ancestry— was overwhelmingly popular. In 1480 the Spanish Inquisition was set up; in 1492 the Jews were told to become Christians or get out; in 1502 the Moors (or Moslems) were told the same. In both cases it was made difficult to leave the country, and even conversion proved to be no protection against further persecution. Thus the national sentiment of Spaniards was colored by a religious and racial element lacking elsewhere in Europe. The fanatical devotion of the Spanish to Catholic Christianity had roots which no Frenchman or Englishman could understand, living as they did in countries which had expelled their Jews two centuries before and knew nothing of Moslems at first hand.

England under the Tudors (1485–1603) went through the

same process of strengthening the royal power which France and Spain underwent, with two significant differences: the foundation of the king's power was not a standing army (England had only one short land frontier to defend against Scotland), but rather popular approval; and as the century progressed the national representative assembly, Parliament, grew in influence while its counterparts, the Estates-General of France and the Cortes of the different Spanish kingdoms, were steadily losing ground.

England was smaller than France and Spain, and class lines and provincial differences were not so deep. Parliament had already become more deeply rooted as a national institution, closely bound up with the monarchy as a focus of English national sentiment. Furthermore, Parliament had a tighter grip on the purse-strings of the nation than the representative assemblies across the channel, and so the ruler had to come to it sooner or later for money, especially in time of war. In moments of national crisis the Tudors felt it necessary to call upon Parliament for support, both material and moral. The result was that Lords and Commons gradually acquired a sense of continuity and of participation in the government which no other representative assembly in Europe had by the close of the century.

The differences between England and her neighboring states should not be exaggerated, however. The main trends were the same. Parliament met seldom enough. The king and his council were the real nerve center of the English government, as of the French and Spanish. Noble blood still counted enormously in English society and government, but both monarchy and middle classes were determined that there should be no repetition of the feudal anarchy and civil war of the preceding century. More and more the actual work of government was carried on by middle-class career men, creatures of the monarchy and therefore willing instruments of royal absolutism. Henry VII (1485–1509) defended his newly founded dynasty against domestic conspiracy and foreign intervention, crushed feudal gangsterism, kept the country out of war, and passed on a full treasury to his son, Henry VIII. The Tudors were generally careful to nurture the English sense of nationality—but not by long exhausting wars on the continent. Thanks to the firm but usually popular policies of the three great Tudors —Henry VII, Henry VIII, and Elizabeth—England was more populous, more prosperous, more united, and more aggressive at the close of the sixteenth century than at the start.

Italy and the Empire

Northern Italy was the cultural center of sixteenth-century Europe. Its cities were wealthier, its industries more advanced, and its trade more flourishing than any other area of comparable size except the Netherlands. By 1500 much of the wealth of its citizens was being devoted to cultural activities. Italian painting, Italian architecture, Italian literature and historical writing, Italian craftsmanship, and Italian business methods—all these were the models of northern countries. The busy, brilliant, hectic life of the Italian city-states is hard to describe in brief compass because of its variety and vitality. Italians were proud of their Roman heritage, proud of their contemporary cultural achievements, contemptuous of northern "barbarians," and yet uneasily aware of their political inferiority to great powers like France. "Italy" was a geographical expression, not a political reality. Five fairly large political units and a host of lesser ones divided the peninsula into small independent principalities and republics of bewildering variety. The kingdom of Naples in the south was something like the western monarchies. The Papal States in the center were unique in that they were the secular possessions of the spiritual head of Christendom, but otherwise they were like other Italian principalities. The dukedom of Milan commanding the Po Valley, the republic of Florence dominating the valley of the Arno, and the republic of Venice at the head of the Adriatic Sea had distinct political personalities of their own.

Italy, it has been said, was a microcosm of the modern world, a kind of social laboratory in which many of the main devices of modern politics and international relations were first tested experimentally. Some of the typical problems of modern politics, such as the conflict of classes and organized pressure groups, first became clear on the small stage of these city-states. Many of the typical devices of modern government such as census-taking, graduated income taxes, and public works programs to meet unemployment were tried out by their governments.

It was perhaps to be expected that the earliest attempt to study political power solely from the point of view of "what is," and not of "what ought to be," was made by an Italian. Niccolo Machiavelli, in exile from his native Florence, wrote the amazing handbook on how to get and keep power which he called *The Prince*, as well as the longer work, *The Discourses*, on why some states endure and grow while others weaken and decline. Italians passed on to the rest of Europe not only artistic and literary models, but also political techniques and speculative hypotheses from their "social laboratory." Together with his contemporary

Guicciardini, Machiavelli formulated some of the shrewdest analysis of power politics ever written and left Europe in debt to Italy for generations. But like the Greek city-states before them, the Italian states were never able to unite or even to federate successfully in the face of threats from great powers outside. To the northern "barbarian," Italy presented the spectacle of great wealth and luxury, superb achievement in the arts, penetrating comment upon the whole gamut of human activity from family life to business and politics—and political fragmentation and frustration.

In the center of Europe was the Holy Roman Empire. The empire was predominantly German, although it was still called Roman and although it included Slavs, Italians, and Netherlanders as well as Germans. The empire was not hereditary, as the western monarchies were; the emperor was elected by the king of Bohemia, the electors of Brandenburg, Saxony, and the Palatinate, and the bishops of Mainz, Trier, and Cologne, all of them powerful princes in their own right. By now the Hapsburgs, whose family holdings were in Austria and the Tyrol, always managed to keep the election in their family. But the imperial title brought only prestige, not power, to its holders. The kingdom of France had a solid core of royal lands attached to the crown, a royal army, a system of national taxation under the control of the king, and a supreme court which served as a court of highest appeal for even the mightiest duke or count. The empire had none of these. At the very end of the fifteenth century a farsighted reformer named Berchtold of Henneberg almost persuaded his fellow electors and the members of the Reichstag (the imperial assembly) to set up an imperial army, revenue system, and supreme court. But Emperor Maximilian himself opposed the scheme and treated

Berchtold as a traitor. As Hapsburg ruler of Austria, Maximilian centralized and strengthened his power much as the kings of the West were doing, but he was too shortsighted to attempt the same job for the empire.

It would have been an almost impossible task in any case. What we today call Germany was a patchwork of practically independent political units of confusing variety: feudal duchies of fair extent but no great power, rich bishoprics ruled by churchmen, wealthy and well-walled cities which acted much like the Italian city-states, and tiny territories, sometimes no more than a castle, ruled by knights who claimed complete autonomy under the emperor. Warfare between these miniature states was almost endemic. One knight had a personal feud with the city of Worms, for instance. He tortured one of the city fathers, diverted the water supply, and cut the roads. A provincial assembly called to deal with him decided it could do nothing, nor could the emperor. The knight stopped causing trouble for a while only when he passed into the service of the king of France. In the end the growing power of the territorial princes curbed feudal anarchy, but as the princes grew stronger the imperial authority grew weaker. Continued weakness at the center and foreign intervention were to lead to the disaster of the Thirty Years' War in the next century.

Since neither the emperor nor the Reichstag could maintain law and order, raise money, and maintain an army, cities sometimes formed alliances with each other for these purposes in order to protect the commerce which was their life blood. The most famous league of cities was the Hanse, a federation of northern German towns now past the peak of its power and influence. A kind of vigilante association called the *Veme* was moderately successful in preserving order in other areas. Such an association formed by townsmen in Castile had been taken over by the crown before 1500 and made an instrument of royal power, but significantly the German emperor was not strong enough to do the same. Dukes, bishops, cities, and knights were a law unto themselves in the empire. What public order there was was either on a very local scale or the result of voluntary associations of towns or individuals.

As a result of these and other factors, there were tensions in Germany more serious than those in any other part of Europe as the century opened. The lot of the peasants was deteriorating in many districts because of a kind of feudal reaction, and there had been some serious peasant rebellions during the fifteenth century. The towns were rich but insecure, ready to grasp at any doctrine or scheme which promised law and order. A vague but palpable national sentiment had been growing among the educated classes for a century, fed on the enthusiasm of a few Humanists for the virtues of the early Germans as described by Tacitus. It was directed not so much against the Turks or the French as against the Roman Church. It could hardly look to the emperor for leadership, since his pretensions and responsibilities were supranational, but it was ready to concentrate upon any other figure who might fire the popular imagination as the defender of a prostrate Germany against the vultures of Rome. Germany was the tinderbox of Europe as the century opened.

Scandinavia, the East, and the Turks

Beyond the eastern half of the circle about Basel already described, there lay a number of sparsely settled states. All of them were influenced in varying degrees by the economic, political, and religious developments at the center of sixteenth-century Europe, but only one of them—the Ottoman Empire—reacted with sufficient vigor to influence Europe to any important degree.

The three Scandinavian monarchies of Denmark, Norway, and Sweden had been formally united under one crown in 1395, but Sweden was already restive and was to assert her independence early in the sixteenth century. Economic and cultural ties between Scandinavia and Germany were close, since the Hanse had dominated Scandinavian trade for two centuries. As the Hanse declined, a native middle class began to appear. The kings of Denmark-Norway and later of Sweden followed much the same policies as the western monarchs in strengthening their own power at the expense of feudal competitors.

In the vast plains of Poland and Lithuania, which were united under the same crown, the story was quite different. A monarchy which had become elective in the previous century was passed around from one princely family of Europe to another and steadily lost what little power it had at the start of the century. Real power in Poland lay with a very numerous and very turbulent nobility, which did everything possible to prevent the rise of a native bourgeoisie and so left trade in the hands of the Jews and the Germans, rigged the Diet (or national assembly) so that it represented only themselves and was incapable of acting against their interests, and ground down the peasantry into a serfdom more intolerable than anything found west of the Elbe. Thus the political and social evolution of Poland was exactly opposite to that of the western monarchies. At the same time there were close cultural ties between the few Polish cities and the rest of Europe, particularly Germany and Italy.

In the grand duchy of Muscovy the consolidation of autocracy and the growth of the idea that Moscow was "the Third Rome" (after Rome herself and Constantinople) provided interesting analogies to the centralization of the western monarchies. But the Russia of Ivan the Terrible (1533–1584) was a long way both physically and spiritually from the England of Elizabeth, even though the two rulers corresponded and exchanged trade missions. Russia was not to make her influence felt appreciably in Europe until another century had gone by.

The presence of the Ottoman Empire astride Asia Minor and the Balkan Peninsula gave Europe what sense of common Christian citizenship it still retained. The Turkish peril to Christendom was at its height in the early sixteenth century. The Ottoman Turks had conquered Constantinople in 1453 and had consolidated their power up to the Danube before the sixteenth century opened. They then turned to the east and south, and conquered parts of Persia, in addition to Syria and Egypt. In 1517 they moved the caliphate from Cairo to Constantinople as a symbol that the religious as well as the political leadership of Islam had passed into their hands. Under their great sultan Suleiman the Magnificent (1520–1566) the pressure against Christian Europe was renewed. In 1520 Belgrade fell; in 1521 Rhodes capitulated. In 1526 the Turkish Janizaries broke a Christian army at Mohacs on the Danube and a thrill of terror ran through European capitals. In 1529 the Turkish army almost captured Vienna. For the next thirty years there was almost continual fighting in Hungary, while an ally of the sultan, Kheireddin Barbarossa, ousted the Spanish from one after another of their strongholds on the north coast of Africa and occasionally raided the coasts of Italy and Spain with his galleys.

The Turkish peril was real. The Janizaries were the best-trained troops in Europe, if not necessarily the best armed. The Turkish genius for war was as well adapted to the sea as to the land. Turkish administration of conquered provinces, at least in comparison with preceding regimes, was so efficient and fair that there seems to have been a disturbing drift of population from Christian states to Turkish territory in the Balkans. The lamentations of scholars about the Turkish threat and the calls to crusades of the popes, therefore, had some justification. But all the evidence suggests that Suleiman did not intend to conquer Christendom, and that he did not have the resources to do so if he had wished. A military equilibrium between Christians and Moslems was established about mid-century, in Hungary and in the Mediterranean, and it was not upset for over a century more. In spite of Suleiman's early victories, the Christians were not so helpless as their writers and propagandists sometimes pictured them to be.

The attitude of Europeans to the Turk was ambiguous. The Venetians and the Hungarians had fought the Turk hard in the fifteenth century, but both were ready at any time to make an advantageous deal with him in order to turn their forces against some Christian enemy. Pope Alexander VI tried to get Turkish support in the face of the French invasion of Italy in 1494. In 1525 the French began a fairly regular policy of going to Constantinople for help whenever the pressure of the Hapsburgs became particularly heavy. The conflict of religious ideology between the Crescent and the Cross was certainly a reality, particularly in countries like Spain and Hungary. But the political and religious differences within Christendom were usually more important than hatred of the Turk in determining the actual policy of any given government at any given time.

The European State System and the Hapsburgs

During the sixteenth century the relationships between the independent and autonomous states which we have described began to assume patterns which were recognizably modern.

The mediaeval conception of a Christendom in which all political units were subdivisions of the *Respublica Christiana*, under the spiritual leadership of the pope and the temporal lordship of the emperor, could still be found in the arguments of diplomatic dispatches, political pamphlets, and religious treatises. The "common corps of Christendom," as Sir Thomas More called it, was still a living reality in men's imaginations. But this conception had long since ceased to correspond very closely with the actual conduct of interstate relations. The real world was the world of practically sovereign, territorial states, competing sharply and constantly with each other for economic advantage, dynastic prestige, national honor, or religious truth.

The monarchs who were so jealous of their power within the boundaries of their states were just as jealous of their independence with respect to other states. "Sovereignty" at home went hand in hand with "sovereignty" abroad. The two were opposite sides of the same political ideal: rightful power over a certain territory with no interference from lesser powers within or greater powers without. This meant that the only law which could govern the relations of sovereign states with each other was the law of the jungle —and Machiavelli came close to saying exactly this. Others were not so clear-sighted or so frank, but the actual policies of rulers were based more and more upon pure "reason of state." This does not mean that the kings were not swayed by irrational motives or outdated ideals like chivalry. They often were. But if the safety of the state or the prestige of the dynasty was at stake, European princes were not scrupulous about the means used to defend their position.

One of the patterns assumed by interstate relations was the maintenance of regular diplomatic contact between governments by means of resident ambassadors. The Italian city-states began the practice in the mid-fifteenth century when the Venetians, the Florentines, the Milanese, and others began to exchange permanent ambassadors who were sent for more than a single *ad hoc* mission. By the early sixteenth century the practice began to spread to the larger states outside Italy until France, Spain, England, and the Holy Roman Empire were maintaining regular representatives at as many as half a dozen other courts. In the techniques of gathering information, evaluating it, and influencing the policy of foreign courts, the Italians—particularly the Venetians—led the way. But the French and Spanish were particularly quick to learn what contemporaries sometimes called the art of privileged spying and lying. *x*

A second pattern was the appearance of a working balance of power. The five leading states of Italy first developed such a balance between themselves in the second half of the fifteenth century. Machiavelli in 1513 duly noted the tacit agreement among the five that no one of them should be allowed to grow so strong as to upset the balance. Actually this miniature system of equilibrium was permanently destroyed when the king of France invaded Italy in 1494 to follow up a dynastic claim to Naples and Milan. This invasion has sometimes been represented as the beginning of modern international politics, and it can be taken so in one sense. During the Italian Wars which followed from 1494 to 1516, one after another of the major European powers was drawn into the conflict until the balance of power, which had once been limited to Italy, began to operate on a European-wide scale.

France was the aggressor in Italy, but Spain was the victor in the long run. The French were unable to make good their rather flimsy dynastic claims to either state, and when Ferdinand of Aragon died in 1516 the Spanish already had a strong foothold in Italy which they steadily consolidated, until the French gave up their Italian expeditions about mid-century. The new and larger balance of power, then, was between the Valois of France and the Hapsburgs of Spain and the empire. The first test of strength came in the Italian Wars (1494–1516), the second in the Hapsburg-Valois Wars (1522–1559). The fact that neither side was able to win a decisive victory in half a century of intermittent fighting was the result partly of limitation of military technology and organization, partly of the half-conscious and awkward efforts of secondary powers like England and the papacy to preserve the balance by shifting their weight at crucial moments to the weaker side.

One of the two major power centers of this new European balance—the French monarchy—has already been described. The other—the large, unwieldy empire of the Hapsburgs —was the product of a curious chain of dynastic accidents.

In 1500 a male child was born to the archduke Philip, heir to the Hapsburg emperor Maximilian (1494–1519), and to Philip's wife Joanna, daughter of Ferdinand and Isabella. It was not exactly planned that this child, who was chris-

Hapsburg = Austria —

tened Charles, should inherit or acquire titles to almost half
of Europe and most of the New World. But the Hapsburgs
were notoriously lucky in their marriages. "Others wage
wars," the saying went, "but you, happy Austria, make
marriages." By the time Charles's grandfather Ferdinand
died in 1516 (Isabella was already dead), several others
(including his own father) who stood between the sixteen-
year-old boy and the crowns of Castile and Aragon had
died, and since his mother Joanna was insane, the boy became King Charles I of Spain, including the Spanish possessions in Italy and America. In 1519 his other grandfather
Maximilian died, and Charles, who was already lord of the
Netherlands, Maximilian's richest acquisition by marriage,
now became ruler of the Hapsburg lands in Austria as well.
That same year, money advanced by the House of Fugger
helped him to be elected emperor as Charles V.

Here was a dynastic empire of startling extent. On paper
at least, the sway of Charles V extended from the Spanish
settlements in the Caribbean, to posts in North Africa and
the western Mediterranean, garrisons in Naples and Milan,
and control of the county of Burgundy and the wealth of
the Netherlands, with the manpower of Spain as the solid
core of the empire. Well might the French think they were
being encircled. If the Hapsburgs should ever gain control
of England, the circle round France would be closed. Early
in the struggle it looked as if the young emperor would
have an easy time of it when he defeated and captured
Francis I, the aggressive and flamboyant king of France, at
Pavia in 1525, took him off to Madrid, and there imposed a
humiliating peace treaty upon him in the next year. But
at this point the balance of power clearly began to operate.
Francis appealed for help to England, the pope, and even

the sultan, and got enough of it to put his country back on even terms by 1529.

This suggests the fact that Charles V's dynastic empire was more impressive on paper than in reality. Upon his election as Holy Roman Emperor in 1519, Charles was told by one of his counselors, "Now that God has given you the prodigious grace of raising you above all kings and princes of Christendom, to such a degree as only Charlemagne among your predecessors ever realized, you are on the road to universal monarchy, on the point of gathering Christendom together beneath a single shepherd." But the road to universal monarchy was a rocky one, and there is not much evidence that the cautious, conscientious, conservative Charles ever really meant to travel it. Actually he spent most of his life fighting against time and distance in a long and weary effort simply to hold together his sprawling inheritance. At the very beginning of his reign in Spain he had to face a serious rebellion. This was hardly quelled when the religious troubles in Germany commanded his attention. Within a year or so he was facing French armies in North Italy, and no sooner were they defeated than the Turkish Janizaries began their terrifying advance up the Danube. For thirty more years until his abdication in 1556, Charles V was like a man desperately trying to extinguish fires in half a dozen different parts of a large forest. In any given two or three years he might be in Barcelona, Tunis, Milan, Augsburg, and Antwerp, traveling by sea because the land routes through France were often closed to him by war, trying wearily to contain the French, to push back the Turk, to settle religious questions which he never quite understood, and to solve the political problems of his conglomerate empire, all more or less simultaneously. It is remarkable that he was as successful as he was in his "sturdy defensiveness," as one historian calls it.

Of the four dominating political personalities of the early sixteenth century—Henry VIII of England (1509–1547), Francis I of France (1515–1547), Suleiman the Magnificent (1520–1566), and Charles V (1519–1556)—Charles was the central figure if only because the ambitions of all the others impinged upon the Hapsburg dominions. In fact, a good biography of Charles is almost a general history of Europe during his lifetime. Nothing illustrates more clearly than this the fact that thanks to the appearance of resident ambassadors, the development of a balance of power, and the presence of the curious dynastic empire of the Hapsburgs, there was now a new sort of unity in Europe. It was not the moral unity of mediaeval Christendom, but rather the troubled sort of unity which we mean today when we speak of "one world." Like the world today, Europe in the sixteenth century was an arena in which independent political powers competed for advantage, a network of political relationships in which a battle, a rebellion, or a heresy anywhere on the continent might have its repercussions everywhere. As Europe lost its spiritual unity, it acquired in return a grim sort of economic and diplomatic unity. ·

The Church

Above all towns and cities, all counties and duchies, all monarchies and even the empire itself, yet reaching down to touch the life of the humblest peasant, was the Roman Catholic Church. It was the one institution common to all of Europe up to the frontiers of Eastern Orthodox Christianity in the East and of Islam in the South. It was the largest and wealthiest institution in Europe, almost impossible to describe in terms of twentieth-century experience.

"Thou art Peter," Jesus had said to the chief of his disciples, "and on this rock [*petros* in Greek] will I found my church." The church was the visible historical institution founded by Christ himself upon Peter and his confession of his Lord's divinity. Peter was reputed to have died in Rome, and succeeding bishops of Rome were taken to be his successors, the vicars of Christ on earth.

The church, then, was a divine, not a human, institution. Yet it was composed of human material—certain human beings set aside from all others to act as ministers of the sacraments and mediators between God and man. These clerics, or "men chosen," were of two kinds: the secular clergy, or priests and bishops, who acted as pastors or shepherds of the flock of Christian laymen; and the regular clergy, or monks and mendicant friars, who lived by a special rule of life which released them from all worldly ties and freed them either for a life of prayer or for a sort of wandering ministry. The paradox of the church from the beginning was that it was a divinely founded institution with the highest purpose—that of mediating God's grace to man through the sacraments and bringing man to salvation in God—and yet an organization inevitably composed of human beings and deeply involved in worldly affairs. This is simply to say that there never was a time when the church was not "corrupt," unworthy of its high purpose, and in need of "reform," if judged by religious standards.

This was particularly true in the early sixteenth century. Not that the abuses were any worse than they had been for a century or two. There are evidences that they were not, that conditions were improving to some extent. Nor was it that the Christian religion was on the wane. The later fifteenth century was, if anything, a period of religious revival. Rather, familiar abuses, such as clerical immorality and the sale of church offices, were now more conspicuous, more talked about, and more resented than they had been. The economic and political changes we have described were having their effect on the church, and new ways of looking at things were encouraging men to regard long-standing abuses in a new light. The church was certainly not in a healthy state. It had lost unity and influence steadily since the height of its prestige in the twelfth and thirteenth centuries. But this was not simply the result of the sins of the priests and monks who composed it. It was not even the result of evil practices and questionable doctrines which had crept into the ecclesiastical organization, though there seemed to be much of this. It was rather the result of a long and slow shifting of social conditions and human values to which the church was not responding readily enough. The sheer inertia of an enormous and complex organization, the drag of powerful vested interests, the helplessness of individuals with intelligent schemes of reform—this is what strikes the historian in studying the church of the later Middle Ages. The church as a human institution had apparently lost its ability to adapt and change and grow.

The main evidence of this was that the church had lost the administrative efficiency and centralization which it had had three centuries earlier. The three key powers of thirteenth-century popes—those of appointment, taxation, and jurisdiction—had been steadily circumscribed in the fifteenth century by the rising national monarchs. Whenever a monarch had pretensions to real sovereignty in his realm, he claimed the right to control the appointment of bishops (whom he often used as his own civil servants in important positions), to limit the amount of money the church could take out of his dominions, and to curtail the appeal of ecclesiastical cases to Rome.

Ferdinand and Isabella went furthest along these lines. By the early sixteenth century they had set up a kind of national church in which the powers of appointment, of taxation, and of ecclesiastical jurisdiction in Castile and Aragon were in effect theirs. In 1516 Francis I of France made a famous and important deal, known as the Concordat of Bologna, with the Medici pope Leo X. This gave the French king almost the same powers that the Catholic kings of Spain had gained, particularly in appointment of the higher clergy, in return for renouncing the doctrine, dear to French hearts for a century, that a church council is superior to the pope. ᵡᵡ In England much the same limitations of papal power had been on the parliamentary statute books since the fourteenth century, but the kings were sometimes inclined to wink at the law and allow the pope somewhat more influence over appointments, somewhat more revenue and jurisdiction, than he was allowed in Spain or France. Between 1515 and 1529 Cardinal Wolsey was able to build up a kind of dictatorship over the English Church with the blessing of both the pope and King Henry VIII. This centralized ecclesiastical power might of course have served to establish full Roman control over the English Church, but it was more likely to serve (as in the end it did) as a model for complete royal control. Strict royal control over national churches was no invention of the sixteenth century. By 1517 the pope's power to appoint, to tax, and to judge had been stringently limited in several nations which (like Spain) were otherwise zealously Catholic.

Significantly there was no such limitation in Germany because there was no secular power strong enough to stand up to the pope. The great bishops in Germany were prince-bishops, ruling wealthy ecclesiastical principalities which were practically independent. The papacy drew a relatively enormous revenue from Germany, in spite of continual and futile complaints from the Imperial Diet or Reichstag about abuses and the burden of ecclesiastical taxation. Unlike the western monarchs, the emperor generally divided the spoil with the pope instead of attempting to stop the flow of gold to Rome. The rising national resentment of the papal powers of appointment, taxation, and jurisdiction in the empire made Germany potentially the most likely scene of revolt against the church in all of Christendom.

There were other limitations on the hierarchical centralization and administrative efficiency of the church beside the pretensions of secular rulers. Many bishops no longer had control either of the monks or of the parish priests within their dioceses. Monastic orders were largely exempt from episcopal jurisdiction, and the appointment of priests was often in the hands of others than the bishop. Most bishops were nobles, with little interest in anything but the revenues and prestige of their position. The gift of a bishopric was a good way for a great lord to provide for a younger son or for a king to support a clever administrator —or his bastard children. Too many bishops held more than one bishopric; many never bothered even to visit their dioceses. The parish clergy—generally poor, ignorant, often indistinguishable from their lay parishioners in mind and morals—were left largely to themselves to administer the sacraments and care for their flock as best they could. The state of the monastic orders varied greatly from order to order and from country to country. But in spite of the genuine zeal and strict discipline of some like the Carthusians, the general trend of monastic piety and morals was downward throughout a good deal of Europe. Even if a reforming bishop or abbot appeared—and there were a few shining examples—he found almost insuperable difficulties in his way because of the general decentralization within the church and the strength of vested interests all down the line.

If reform was to come at all, apparently it could come only from the top, from the papacy itself. But the papacy of the Renaissance was a most unlikely source of reform. In 1500 the worst of all the popes was on the papal throne, Alexander VI, indulgent father of the notorious Cesare Borgia and benefactor of hordes of rapacious relatives from Spain. Under Alexander the immorality, the venality, and the conspicuous spending which had already made the papal court a by-word among those who knew Rome reached their height. Typically, the contributions which flowed in from the faithful all over Europe during the jubilee year of 1500 went mostly to help Cesare carve out a principality for himself in central Italy. There were reformers at the Vatican, but they were helpless because any real reform which was proposed had the effect of cutting down the papal revenues, and this promptly sent panic through the host of officials and hangers-on who made up the cumbrous machinery of papal government.

The Sacred and the Secular: Indulgences

This brings us to the heart of the problem of the condition of the church. The papacy of the early sixteenth century was only one step ahead of bankruptcy a good deal of the time. The necessity of defending the papal states (and the desire to enlarge them), the burden of supporting an elaborate administrative organization (and a luxurious court), the obligation to support anti-Turkish crusades (and perhaps also wars against papal enemies closer to home in France, Germany, or Italy)—all this cost money. This money was squeezed out of the higher clergy in various ways, particularly by what was called simony, or the sale of spiritual offices. But the clergy had in the end to squeeze the money out of the producing classes in society, the peasants and artisans, the merchants and professional people. Rents were raised on the enormous holdings of church lands, and fees were increased for spiritual services performed by the clergy. In the end the squeeze imposed by the papacy on the higher clergy was passed on to the laity in the form of higher charges by the parish clergy for everything from burials and the probate of wills to administration of the sacraments themselves.

The practice of issuing indulgences in return for "contributions" from the faithful is the best illustration of how a hard-pressed papacy was tempted to trade spiritual benefits for hard cash. An indulgence was originally a remission of the "penance," or temporal penalty for sin, imposed by the priest in the sacrament of penance. Indulgences were granted by papal dispensation to crusaders, to pilgrims, and finally to any who contributed to some such cause as building a church. Indulgences were very lucrative. The revenue which they brought into the papal treasury was greatly increased in the fifteenth century by the popular belief that an indulgence could not only assure divine forgiveness of sins with a minimum of contrition, but also release the souls of the dead from Purgatory. The best teaching of the church insisted upon the necessity of full contrition and was very cautious about asserting the pope's power over Purgatory. But extravagant claims were made for the papal power by some. During the fifteenth century it became official dogma that there was a treasury of superfluous merits accumulated by Christ and the saints, and that the church could dispense these merits to the buyers of indulgences. In this as in so many other contemporary practices—including the veneration of saints and relics, pilgrimages, and the administration of the sacraments themselves—the line between the spiritual and the material became blurred in the eyes of many ordinary believers. The church was trading upon its monopoly of the means of salvation in order to raise money for largely secular purposes, or so it seemed to increasing numbers of laymen and conscientious clergymen. The sacred and the secular were inextricably confused in innumerable ways and at every level in ecclesiastical practice.

Many Catholic writers put the whole blame for this general situation on the "greed, thirst for power, and lusts of the flesh" of secular rulers who sabotaged every attempt at reform. Many Protestant writers tend to blame the same faults in clergymen, from the pope down. Clearly one must look deeper for the underlying causes—in the economic expansion, the growing need for political consolidation, and the increasing worldliness of taste and thought both within and outside the clergy. The impulse to be a Christian was probably as strong in as many people then as it had been three centuries earlier, but disturbing and half-formulated questions were occurring to many people. What was it to be a Christian? To buy an indulgence? To become a monk? Or to read the Bible and live a good life? Was a great supranational organization centered in Rome a necessary part of Christianity? Was a mediating priesthood necessary to represent the divine power on earth, and were the sacraments the only channels of God's grace to man? Not one of these questions was new, but unless reform could be accomplished, they would grow in urgency and poignancy.

Conceptions of Reform

Before Luther appeared on the scene there were four main theories of how the church might be reformed.

The first looked to saintly individuals to spread new life through the church by the contagion of their example. This conception was based upon a conviction widely held in the Middle Ages that institutions were patterned by God and so could not be made better or worse. Therefore the proper approach was to pray for the conversion of individuals rather than to attempt the futile task of reorganizing the church as an institution. This was the hope of the great mystics of the later Middle Ages. It was the guiding conception of the Dominican friar Savonarola in his brief and tragic attempt to call the city of Florence to repentance, as preacher, prophet, and political leader of the city from 1494 to his execution in 1498. There was much to be said for the proposition that without individual conversion no ecclesiastical reform would be possible. But the mystics and the prophets of the fifteenth century who conceived of reform in these terms had been singularly helpless in the face of the deeply entrenched evils which they deplored and denounced.

In contrast, the second conception of reform was strongly institutional. It was the conciliar theory, the theory that since the papacy itself was corrupt, a general council representing the church as a whole should shoulder the burden of reform. In spite of the failure of the Councils of Constance (1414–1418) and of Basel (1431–1449) either to reform the church or to make good their authority over the popes, the conciliar theory still had wide appeal in the sixteenth century. It rested upon the belief that while parts of the church and even the papacy itself might be utterly corrupt, God's truth and grace were preserved in the church as a whole, in the "whole company of the faithful." Twentieth-century democratic faith that the common man remains uncorrupted in spite of the politicians who prey upon him has something in common with this conciliar theory. But there was surprisingly little real foundation for such optimism about the beneficial results of setting up a limited, constitutional monarchy in the church. Secular rulers had acquired the habit of using an appeal to a council as a club to hold over the pope, in order to gain purely secular advantages. In reply the pope was apt to summon a subservient and unrepresentative council (as Julius II did in 1512) merely to head off the threat from secular monarchs. No wonder that the attitude of many toward reform by a general council was compounded of both hope and despair.

The third conception of reform was that it should be carried out by the secular rulers. This was the most illogical conception of the three, but probably the most widespread. It was always assumed in mediaeval theory that the secular ruler had a wide responsibility for defending and protecting the church. Conscientious emperors and kings often assumed that this included the duty of aiding or even initiating ecclesiastical reforms. As the secular rulers of Europe grew more powerful in their dominions, "reforming" everything from feudal anarchy to business practices and personal dress, it was perhaps natural that more and more of their subjects should look to them as the real image of God's power on earth and therefore the proper castigators of a corrupt clergy. This theory appealed to all those who feared the wealth and power of the clergy, whether for disinterested or selfish reasons. It formed common theoretical ground on which the sincere religious reformer and the rapacious ruler with a hungry eye on church lands could meet, at least for a time. There was of course no guarantee that a monarch would be any more zealous for real ecclesiastical reform than a pope. But the monarch's interest, both public and private, usually lay on the side of reform. At least he had no vested interest in the financial abuses of the church—quite the contrary. The most outstanding example of successful reform in the early years of the sixteenth century was that accomplished by Cardinal Ximenes de Cisneros, who stamped out some of the worst abuses and made strenuous efforts to raise the educational level of the clergy in Spain. The success of Ximenes' efforts in Spain was made possible by the strong backing he received from Ferdinand and Isabella, not by any impetus received from the Vatican. It appeared that wherever there was a strong monarch, reform was at least possible. Where the national ruler was weak as in Germany, reform seemed almost hopeless.

Christian Humanism

The fourth conception of reform was newer and therefore more exciting than any of the others to many of the best minds in Europe. It was the program of a group of scholars whom we now call Christian Humanists. The essence of it was that the new learning would save the church.

As scholars gradually restored direct contact with the best in classical and early Christian thought, so the Christian

Humanists believed, the church would inevitably be cleansed
and invigorated. To read the dialogues of Plato and the
epistles of Paul in the original Greek was to recover the
greatness and simplicity of the Greek ideal and the Christian
Gospel, obscured for centuries by the arid and undiscerning
commentaries of theologians who never read the original
texts. No wonder abuses and false doctrine had crept in.
The church had lost touch with its roots in the religion of
Palestine and the civilization of Greece and Rome. What
was needed, the Christian Humanists insisted, was to publish
the original texts of the Greek philosophers, the Biblical
writers, and the early Fathers of the Christian church, to
study them afresh as human documents which speak straight
to the heart, and to base the education of the younger generation, particularly the rulers, on these classics of western
thought rather than on the narrow scholastic learning of the
past few centuries. The result would be assured. The way
to men's wills and hearts is through their minds. As men
came to know the good through such an education, they
would do the good. The saintliness of Socrates and the
simple religion of Jesus himself, the "philosophy of Christ,"
would so move men by contrast with the mechanistic religious practices of some fifteen centuries later that abuses
would simply wither away. Who would buy an indulgence
if he knew that what God demands is not sacrifice and
sacrament but a humble and a contrite heart? Who would
split theological hairs and burn heretics if he realized that
the essence of Christianity is to lead a Christlike life?

  The authors of this program included the Italian Pico
della Mirandola, the Frenchman Lefèvre d'Étaples, the
Spaniard Luis Vives, the Englishman Sir Thomas More
(statesman as well as scholar), and the acknowledged leader

of them all, Erasmus of Rotterdam. Erasmus was the soul
of the movement. A first-rate scholar and enthusiastic lover
of the classics, he became slowly converted to an ambitious
calling, that of saving Christendom through Christian scholarship. He did yeoman service to the cause of reform by
his learning, his intelligence, his humor, and his tolerant
understanding. He had the honor of being the first actually
to publish the New Testament in the original Greek (1516),
although Cardinal Ximenes and fellow scholars in Spain
were already far along on their great edition of the whole
Bible in the original Hebrew and Greek. He edited the first
scholarly editions of many of the Fathers, and in a scholarly
joke called *The Praise of Folly,* he ridiculed some of the
worst abuses among the clergy as seen from the point of
view of a simple ethical Christianity strongly flavored with
Platonism.

Erasmus represented the best in Christian Humanism—its
faith in man's reason and fundamental goodness, its confidence in education, its tolerance and sense of proportion.
He also illustrated many of its weaknesses. Most of its leaders
(except Sir Thomas More) were scholars and writers, but
not men of affairs. It was perhaps natural therefore that
they exaggerated the power of the pen and the importance
of scholarship. There was something contagious about their
enthusiasm for what they found in the newly read sources
of Greek and Christian tradition, but the contagion could
not be expected to spread very far down in society. Eras-
mian reformers were scattered in key positions in the church
throughout Europe, and their scholarship and their ideas
had important influence on more dogmatic reformers as far
apart as Luther and Loyola. But their program proved to
be too reasonable, too mild, too unmindful of the radical

evil in human nature, to triumph. Like the "philosophers" of the eighteenth century, they gave their contemporaries a new perspective from which to criticize ancient abuses and outworn ideas. The fact that abuses were so talked about and deplored was largely their work. They looked at sixteenth-century practices through the eyes of the disciples of Socrates and of Jesus. In so doing they presented their readers and listeners with a vague but stirring alternative to the contemporary state of affairs—and without an alternative in men's minds to the status quo, revolutions are never possible. Like the philosophers of the Enlightenment, however, they were generally shocked by the form which revolution actually took. When Europe became divided between Catholic and Protestant, the Christian Humanists remained Catholic almost to a man.

As so often in human affairs, the actual form taken by the major reform movements of the sixteenth century was not a simple incarnation of any one of these four conceptions, which have just been distinguished with artificial sharpness. In varying degrees, all four conceptions had their influence on both Protestant and Catholic Reformations. But the actual historical form which Protestantism took was to a large extent unexpected, unprecedented, and therefore unique.

CHAPTER II

The Religious Upheaval

THE immediate origins of the Protestant Reformation lay in the religious experience of Martin Luther (1483–1546). We will never know precisely what happened to Luther in the years between his becoming a monk in 1505 and his dramatic attack on indulgences in 1517. But we know from his contemporary lecture notes and from his later writings and conversations with friends that he underwent years of harrowing emotional and intellectual tension which finally resulted in a "conversion" experience sometime during these years. The nature of this experience was to determine the main features of Protestant belief and the direction which the Protestant movement took. It is important, therefore—difficult as it is—to sketch briefly the inner struggles of this obscure Augustinian friar and their outcome.

Salvation by Faith

Outwardly, young Martin Luther was one of the most pious and diligent monks in the friary at Erfurt. "If ever a monk got to heaven by his monkery," he wrote twenty years later, "I should certainly have got there." But he was haunted from the beginning by doubts about whether he, a mere man and a sinner, could ever satisfy a righteous God.

In spite of fastings, scourgings, and prayer beyond the rule, he could gain no sense of being forgiven. Doubt aroused fear, and fear led to moments of panic and despair. Staupitz, the kindly vicar of the order, could not understand this sensitive and intelligent younger brother who was constantly confessing his minor sins and yet could never quite rid himself of the sense of guilt.

Scholars differ in explaining Luther's predicament. Perhaps his conception of God as a stern and righteous Judge owed something to the character of his father, a hard-working peasant and miner, devoted to his son's welfare but strict and demanding. Perhaps it owed something to stern representations of God in either sculpture or story impressed upon him at an early age. He had taken the vow to become a monk in a moment of panic during a thunderstorm, and the fact that he immediately regretted it but went through with it may have contributed to his later tension. Luther was a high-strung person with keen sensibilities and a sensitive conscience, not the kind to persuade himself easily that he was doing the best he could and that the rest might be left to God (as his spiritual advisers urged). The theological school which dominated the teaching at the University of Erfurt where he had studied put strong emphasis on what were called "good works," a term which included sacramental and ceremonial acts (such as doing penance, fasting, going on a pilgrimage, entering a monastery) as well as acts of charity. The kernel of this teaching was that man through his own effort and will has a large share in determining his ultimate salvation or damnation. In effect, Luther was acting on this teaching, but failing miserably to gain any inner assurance of forgiveness and so of the promise of salvation.

Then something happened. In 1511 Staupitz had seen that Luther was appointed Professor of Bible at the new University of Wittenberg, and for a year or more the thirty-year-old professor had been soaking himself in Scripture. The influence of his friends and his reading began to suggest a solution to his soul's plight. As he remembered it later, it all happened suddenly (some scholars think in the winter of 1512–1513) in the tower room of the Augustinian friary at Wittenberg where he lived, perhaps while he was writing notes for his lectures on the Psalms (which scholars rediscovered only a half-century ago). Here is his own account, written in 1545, of his attempt to probe St. Paul's meaning in Romans 1:17:

> After I had pondered the problem for days and nights, God took pity on me and I saw the inner connection between the two phrases, "The justice of God is revealed in the Gospel" and "The just shall live by faith." I began to understand that this "justice of God" is the righteousness by which the just man lives through the free gift of God, that is to say "by faith."
> . . . Thereupon I felt as if I had been born again and had entered Paradise through wide-open gates. Immediately the whole of Scripture took on a new meaning for me. I raced through the Scriptures, so far as my memory went, and found analogies in other expressions.[1]

Luther felt he had rediscovered the meaning of St. Paul's conviction that a Christian is saved not by moral or ceremonial "works," but by his faith in the loving and merciful Father who incarnated Himself in Jesus Christ in order to

[1] Preface to Luther's Collected Works 1545, trans. by E. Harris Harbison in Kenneth M. Setton and Henry R. Winkler, eds., *Great Problems in European Civilization* (New York: Prentice-Hall, Inc., 1954), pp. 252–253.

save men. This faith is a "free gift of God." Salvation cannot be deserved or merited, then; it cannot be bought or bargained for by the doing of good works—by fastings and prayer, penances and pilgrimages, or even by becoming a monk. No man can fulfill God's requirements and thus become righteous because all men are sinners, but God counts man's faith (which is His own free gift to man) as the equivalent of righteousness. Luther had tried and failed to merit forgiveness and salvation. At the moment of blackest despair he realized that in the saving of souls literally everything is God's work and nothing is man's. Salvation is the free gift of a loving God to undeserving man.

Scripture and Conscience

Luther was not a systematic or logical thinker. Rather, his thinking was existential, that is, it developed out of his own personal experience and the decisions he had to make in living out his own life. If he had been more logically inclined, he might have concluded immediately that if a Christian is saved by his faith alone, then the whole mediaeval church, with its sacraments and ceremonies, its papacy and its priesthood, was really unnecessary. A man alone in his room with God and God's Word, the Bible, like Luther in his tower room—this would be the true picture of a Christian—not that of a man confessing his sins to a priest, traveling on a pilgrimage, or buying an indulgence to get his dead parents out of Purgatory. This was to be the heart of Protestant belief as it developed later: the Bible and a man's conscience are the channels through which God speaks to human beings, not the Roman Church and its sacraments. But it took personal contact with the practice of indulgences, and later the attacks of enemies, to make Luther realize the full implications of his own religious experience. And even to the end, he never broke with what he thought was the *true* Church of Christ and its sacraments. ✗

The Mainz Indulgence of 1515 was a peculiarly lurid example of the connection between spiritual and financial abuses in the church. The pope proclaimed an indulgence ostensibly to raise money for the building of St. Peter's in Rome. Actually all but a very small percentage of the money raised found its way into the pockets of the Dominican monks who sold the coveted certificates to the people, of bankers who handled the receipts, and of a great ecclesiastical prince, Albert of Hohenzollern, who owed the pope a large bribe for the privilege of holding three bishoprics when the canon law said that no one might hold more than one. Luther, like the ordinary person, knew nothing of Albert's deal with the pope. He knew only that his students at the University of Wittenberg were flocking across the border of Saxony to buy indulgences in Magdeburg and returning to him convinced that their sins were forgiven. John Tetzel, a particularly unscrupulous Dominican, was preaching to the crowds that "so soon as coin in coffer rings, the soul from Purgatory springs." In indignation born of his own religious experience, Luther drafted 95 Theses attacking the current doctrine of indulgences. The most radical proposition was that "Any Christian whatever, who is truly repentant, enjoys full remission from penalty and guilt, and this is given him without letters of indulgence."

Luther probably had no intention of doing more than start an academic debate on his theses at the University of Wittenberg. But it became evident almost overnight that he had touched on the most sensitive nerve of the whole ecclesiastical organization of his day. The theses were published and devoured by Germans everywhere. The pent-up resentment against papal exactions and ecclesiastical abuses became polarized by his attack. The sale of indulgences fell off sharply, and the Dominicans demanded that Luther be curbed. Step by step, opponents who saw the doctrinal and financial dangers in Luther's criticisms forced him to work out the implications of his position. First he appealed to the pope, but the Medici Leo X was inclined to treat the whole matter as an unimportant quarrel between monks. When Leo's attitude became harder, he appealed from the pope to a general council. Finally a particularly skillful debater, Dr. John Eck, manoeuvred him into declaring that even a general council was fallible—which left him with Scripture and conscience as his only ultimate authorities. This became perfectly clear when he faced the emperor Charles V and the assembled Diet of the empire at Worms in 1521 and replied to the demand that he recant his views with words which were to become famous throughout Europe:

Unless I am convinced by the evidence of Scripture or by plain reason—for I do not accept the authority of the Pope or the councils alone, since it is established that they have often erred and contradicted themselves—I am bound by the Scriptures I have cited and my conscience is captive to the Word of God. I cannot and will not recant anything, for it is neither safe nor right to go against conscience. God help me. Amen.

Protestant Beliefs

Between 1520, when Luther wrote the tracts and pamphlets which are still the best expression of his religious ideas, and 1530, when the beliefs of the church he founded were summarized in the Augsburg Confession, the main lines of Protestant belief and practice were worked out by Luther himself and his lieutenants in Wittenberg, with some contributions from independent leaders of revolt against Rome such as Ulrich Zwingli in Zurich and Martin Bucer in Strasbourg.

The best general description of Protestantism [2] is still probably that of Ernst Troeltsch: "A modification of Catholicism, in which the Catholic formulation of problems was retained, while a different answer was given to them." In particular, Luther offered relatively new answers to four questions which go far back in Christian history. To the question how is a man to be saved, Luther answered: not by works but by faith. To the question where does religious authority lie, he answered: not in the visible institution known as the Roman Church, but in the "Word of God" contained in the Bible. To the question what is the church, he answered: the whole community of Christian believers, since all are really priests and since every man must be "a Christ to his neighbor." To the question what is the essence of Christian living, he replied: serving God in one's calling, whether secular or ecclesiastical, since all useful callings are equally sacred in the eyes of God. These were the four central Protestant beliefs, each closely related to the others: salvation by faith rather than by works, the authority of the Bible interpreted by the consecrated conscience, the priest-

[2] "Protestant" was a kind of nickname given to a group of Lutheran princes who presented a "protest" against repressive measures at an Imperial Diet in 1529. The name stuck and is generally applied today to all non-Catholic, non-Orthodox Christians, although it should perhaps be limited historically to the six major families of Protestant denominations: Lutheran, Anglican, Calvinist (Reformed or Presbyterian), Congregationalist, Baptist, and Methodist. This would exclude Unitarian groups. But it is impossible to be absolutely precise in use of the term. The quotation that follows is from *Protestantism and Progress* (New York, 1912), p. 59.

hood of all believers, and the service of God in secular as well as clerical callings. All could be taken to follow from Luther's original experience of God's saving grace in the gift of faith.

To sixteenth-century followers of Luther, Protestantism was essentially a *restoration*. During the Middle Ages—so the theory ran—Christianity had become encrusted and overloaded with doctrines and practices which had nothing to do with its essence and which came close to obliterating the Gospel revealed to the early church. It was imperative to go back to Paul and the Gospels, back to the practices and insights of the Apostolic Age, in order to recapture Christian truth. The canon law and scholastic theology of recent centuries were satanic corruptions of the primitive Gospel. The bishop of Rome, far from representing Christ on earth, was the Anti-Christ prophesied in the Book of Revelation.

To sixteenth-century Catholics, Protestantism was essentially a *revolution*. To deny that Christ had founded his church on Peter and that the popes were Peter's successors, to question the divine institution of the seven sacraments, to say that all believers are equally priests, that all men are saved or damned by the arbitrary will of God with no respect to good works or merit—all this was either heresy or blasphemy to loyal sons of the mediaeval church. Luther, not Leo, was the Anti-Christ—the "wild boar" which was ravaging God's vineyards, in the words of the papal bull which excommunicated the heretic friar in 1520.

Today most historians refer to Protestantism as a *reformation*. In the ordinary sense of moral reform, Protestantism probably accomplished little. Nor did Luther think of his movement as aimed primarily at the improvement of clerical and lay morality. Protestantism is properly described, however, as a reforming or reformulating of the Christian tradition. In attempting to restore first-century Christianity, the early Protestants were inevitably revolutionists. In going back, they moved forward. And the result was that they gave a new shape to the Christian tradition in almost half of Europe.

The Appeal of Protestantism

One of the most difficult tasks of the historian is to discover how and why a complex set of ideas like those of Luther captures men's minds and so becomes a historical "movement." The simplest explanation is to say that Luther was a "typical" German of his day, with an uncanny feeling for the religious problems of ordinary people, and that his teachings went straight to the hearts of those who were tired as he was of trying to win salvation by good works. There is truth in this, but as an explanation it obviously applies only to a tiny minority of persons who had a religious sensibility and sophistication comparable to Luther's. What of the many others all over Europe—peasants, artisans, merchants, lawyers, priests, monks, and princes—who we know became "Lutherans"?

Among the lowest classes there were many who misinterpreted Luther to mean that God meant men to be free of *all* bonds, social and economic as well as ecclesiastical. They were soon disillusioned when Luther made it clear that what he meant by "the liberty of a Christian" was freedom from the galling restrictions of the Roman Church, not freedom from serfdom or from obedience to secular rulers. But they were awakened and thrilled, nevertheless, by Luther's heroic defiance of authority.

Much has been written about the appeal of Protestantism

to the middle classes. The tendency of recent scholarship is to be cautious about generalization on the subject. But Lutheran and particularly Calvinist teachings certainly had special appeal to the merchants and professional people of Europe, particularly in the North. These were the classes which had obvious reasons to dislike papal taxation, to envy the church's wealth, and to despise the luxury and corruption of the nonproductive bishops and monks. Salvation by faith alone, the priesthood of all believers, and serving God in one's calling were attractive slogans to such people— sometimes, but not always, for the purely religious reasons Luther himself would have wished. Not that the ordinary bourgeois was irreligious. More often he was a person deeply immersed in secular pursuits—building up a business, amassing wealth, carrying on a law practice, or serving a monarch —troubled in conscience by the gulf between his worldly interests and the other-worldly ideal imbued in him by the Roman Church. For this reason he might be much attracted by the idea that a man is saved by faith, not by sacramental magic and the buying of indulgences, and that one can serve God just as well as a merchant or magistrate as one can by being ordained priest or monk. Who can estimate the subtle balance of religious and secular motives in the souls of such persons, to whom Lutheranism meant an answer to the question how they might gain salvation and still remain fully in the active world of business competition and human pleasure?

To the German governing classes, the prospects of curbing the independent power of the supranational church in their particular dominions, of establishing control over the local clerical hierarchy, of possibly confiscating the lands of monasteries and even bishoprics, had particular appeal.

In 1520 Luther appealed to "the ruling class of the German people" to reform the church, since the church would not reform itself. Such an appeal to the secular rulers was nothing new, as we have seen, but it had decisive results for the Lutheran movement. Luther was a peasant and a monk, naturally inclined to think in terms of authority and obedience to lawfully constituted powers. He turned to the princes and magistrates for support, and he was not disappointed. Before his death in 1546 he saw duchy after duchy and city after city in north and central Germany break with Rome, subordinate the local church to the state, dissolve the monasteries, and simplify the church services, all under the leadership and usually at the instigation of the ruling prince or the town council. Luther himself had no intention to preach the "divine right of kings," but the circumstances in which he found himself, together with his own instincts, led him to rely on the powers that be to defend the Gospel. Most of the German rulers who took up his challenge to reform the church profited considerably in terms of political power and wealth.

One element in the appeal of Protestantism to all classes of European society, particularly in Germany, was national sentiment. The drain of ecclesiastical taxation was particularly severe in Germany because there was no strong national ruler to stand up against it and the unimpeded abuse was correspondingly resented. This resentment played no part in Luther's own early development, but soon after his attack on indulgences he sensed the support he was receiving from German national sentiment and learned to play upon it. The papacy was wealthy, corrupt—and Italian. It was intolerable, he wrote in 1520, that the pope and cardinals should mulct his countrymen and then refer contemptuously to them as "silly drunken Germans." "If the kingdom of France has resisted it, why do we Germans let the Romanists make fools and monkeys of us in this way?" The appeal of Protestantism to national patriotism was perhaps strongest in Germany, but national sentiment was also a major factor in the appeal of Protestantism to Scandinavians, Englishmen, Netherlanders, and some Frenchmen.

National sentiment is intimately related to language. Within twenty years of the publication of Erasmus' Greek New Testament in 1516 with its preface urging the translation of Scripture into the common tongues of Europe, there were new versions of the Bible in German, French, and English which were to play an important part in the growth of both national sentiment and of Protestant conviction. In 1526 Tyndale began, and in 1535 Coverdale completed a new English version of the Bible which was a steppingstone to the King James Version of 1611, the most influential of all books in the forming of the English mind in the next century. By 1535 there were two new French versions, one in the Catholic spirit by Lefèvre d'Etaples, one in the Protestant by Olivétan. Luther's matchless German Bible, begun in 1522 and completed in 1532, was the greatest of them all if measured by the vigor and vitality of its style and by its influence on a people. Everywhere Protestants became "People of the Book," in an English historian's phrase. The effect of translating the Scriptures into the vulgar tongues was enormous. In an age which knew no television, radio, or even newspapers, the impact of the imagery and wisdom of the Bible upon those able to read their own language was almost revolutionary. In addition to the Bible, theological controversy was carried to the reading public in thousands of printed tracts (Luther's great appeals of 1520,

Calvin's own French translation of his *Institutes* in 1541, for example). Cartoons concentrated and focused the gist of the printed word. Services in Protestant churches were conducted in the common tongue. Prayer itself, as a French historian puts it, was "nationalized."

Such were some of the elements, religious and secular, relevant and irrelevant, in the appeal of Protestantism to ordinary people in Germany and elsewhere in Europe. We shall consider the mentality of those to whom Protestantism did not appeal in treating the Catholic Reformation.

The Spread of Lutheranism to 1546

It was partly converted persons, partly printed books and pamphlets, that spread Luther's ideas. Naturally Luther's students and fellow professors at Wittenberg were his first converts, and to the end of his life the university was the nerve center of what came to be called "Lutheranism." The faculty of the university was solidly behind him when he posted his 95 Theses, and his colleagues were his staunchest early supporters, even if some like Melancthon became more conservative, some like Carlstadt more radical, than their leader. After a sharp drop in the 1520's following Luther's excommunication, student enrollment rose steadily at the university, reaching a peak in the 1540's and 1550's. Between 1520 and 1560 some sixteen thousand students went to Wittenberg from all over Germany, returning home as often as not to spread Luther's ideas. Priests and monks were particularly likely to be among the early converts, in addition to students and their families.

Luther's writings in both German and Latin, spread by the printing press, reached others not reached by converted Lutherans. The primary appeal of his thought was limited to Germans and Scandinavians, but his Latin writings were circulated and read in the Netherlands, England, France, Poland, Switzerland, and even in Spain and Italy in the 1520's and 1530's.

Wittenberg was not the only radiating center of Lutheran ideas, however, even if it was the most important till almost mid-century. Zurich (after 1523) and Strasbourg (after 1525) were also important centers of Protestant activity in the same period.

Ulrich Zwingli (1484–1531) was the leader of reform in Zurich. He was a secular priest and man of affairs, both more practical and more systematic a reformer than Luther. Logical, even rationalistic, in his thinking and puritanical in his moral attitudes, he was much more directly influenced by Erasmus and the Christian Humanists than was Luther. Although his career as a reformer had begun before he had heard of Luther, it was Luther's writings that provided the decisive influence in his development, and he came to share most of Luther's basic beliefs. But the two reformers eventually (1529) came to an irreconcilable disagreement on whether Christ was truly present in the sacrament of Holy Communion or not. Luther maintained the Real Presence and Zwingli argued that the sacrament was essentially a memorial of the Last Supper. This was the first of the long succession of schisms within Protestantism which were to make its history at the same time so dynamic and so tragic.

Martin Bucer (1491–1551), a more irenic person with something of both Luther and Zwingli in him, tried unsuccessfully but heroically to make Strasbourg the bridge between Wittenberg and Zurich. Under his leadership Strasbourg remained the most tolerant Protestant city in Europe until the late 1530's, a haven for religious refugees of every description. Bucer's belief in predestination and in the moral supremacy of church over state influenced Calvin, who lived in Strasbourg from 1538 to 1541; and his compromise position that the body of Christ was truly present in the sacrament of Holy Communion, but only to the believing soul, influenced Thomas Cranmer and the English Prayer Book. So Strasbourg was a third important center of Protestant influence in the period before Luther's death.

To a pious Catholic, the steady spread of the Lutheran heresy in central Europe in the three decades between the 95 Theses (1517) and the death of Luther (1546) was as frightening as the spread of Nazi power after 1933 or of Soviet power after 1945 was to the democratic world. The story was much the same in town after town. A Lutheran preacher would arrive, or a local priest would become converted. Soon there were murmurings against the Mass, public debates between defenders of the old and new, perhaps some breaking of images of the saints in the churches. Then would come a petition to the town council to abolish the Mass, possibly accompanied by more violence. In the end the Mass would be abolished, a simpler service substituted with congregational singing and regular catechizing, and the clergy would marry and become servants of the state rather than of Rome. Monasteries would usually be "secularized," the revenues going to the secular government and the inmates being forced out into secular life.

The great free cities of western Germany were the first to go: Augsburg, Nuremberg, Strasbourg, and Hamburg went Lutheran almost before the echoes of Luther's defiance of the emperor at Worms in 1521 had died away. Zurich abolished the Mass in 1525, Basel in 1529. Then territorial rulers began to follow suit. Till his death in 1525 Luther's own ruler, the elector of Saxony, cautiously protected the reformer, and then his successor openly adopted Luther's reforms. By 1530 Hesse, Prussia, Denmark, and Sweden had also been added to the list of Lutheran territories. In that year the Lutherans drafted a creed, the Augsburg Confession, and in the next year a defensive alliance of Protestant states was formed. The most important accession to Lutheran strength in Germany during the 1530's was Brandenburg, but the most crucial addition to Protestant strength in general came when the English king and Parliament formally severed connection with Rome in 1534 (see below). The last serious attempt to heal the breach in western Christendom was made at Ratisbon in 1541, when leading Protestants and Catholics met in a vain attempt to discover a formula which would provide common ground for both sides. By 1546, when Luther died, Germany was hopelessly divided between Lutheran and Catholic states and on the verge of religious war; England and Scandinavia were lost to the papacy; and Lutheran doctrines were apparently spreading in the Netherlands and in the towns of northern France. The movement to reform the church had resulted in a schism far more dangerous to the unity of Catholic Christianity than any since the final separation between Roman and Eastern Orthodox Christianity in 1054.

The Left Wing

To religious conservatives, as we have noted, Lutheranism looked like unbounded revolution. To some in Europe, however, Luther appeared to be a conservative if not a reactionary at heart, who had misled the people by beckoning them forward against the foe and then suddenly calling a halt. These were the religious radicals, men who believed the old order was corrupt to the very roots. In spite of all Luther's talk about salvation by faith alone, the authority of the Word, and the priesthood of all believers, the Lutheran churches retained an ordained clergy who administered the sacraments of Baptism and Holy Communion, who considered the whole population of a given territory members of their church, and who looked to the state for salary and support. In other words, the Lutheran churches were still "established churches." To those in the "left wing" of the movement, all this was a betrayal of what was really revolutionary in Luther's teaching. Some of them perhaps unconsciously looked back to mediaeval heretical traditions which had emphasized hatred of the clergy, the authority of Scripture, and puritanical fear of any compromise with worldliness. In any case, these radicals felt that official Protestantism was not much better than mediaeval Catholicism. They agreed with Luther that what was needed was a restoration of the beliefs and practices of the early church, but they saw in the Lutheran churches simply a caricature of the ideal. One of their favorite words was "restitution," by which they meant literally turning the clock back to the first century and restoring the spirit and institutions of the Apostolic Age.

These radicals were generally called "Anabaptists," meaning persons who believed in "rebaptism," which had been condemned as heresy ten centuries before in Justinian's Code. But they called themselves simply "Baptists," meaning that they thought infant baptism no sacrament at all and adult baptism the only true test of membership in the Christian church. It was their conception of the church which was their most characteristic and most influential belief. The Christian church, they insisted, is a voluntary association of believers who have experienced spiritual regeneration and have been baptized into membership—as the early Christians were—as adults. The church is not identical with society at large, as Luther and Calvin, no less than the pope himself, insisted it was. It is a "gathered" church, a company of saints (and therefore a minority), a holy community subject to strict entrance requirements and strenuous discipline. It is a light set upon a hill, a candle shining in a naughty world. Like the monasteries of the Middle Ages, the Anabaptist church was to influence society by the example of its purity—and its martyrdom. Unlike the monks, its members remained laymen and married, but they often cut themselves strictly off from the world, sometimes to the point of refusing to bear arms, to hold political office, or to take an oath. Conversely they stoutly maintained that the state has no rightful power over religion and that the secular magistrate must keep his hands off the church.

Within Anabaptist churches a strict sort of democracy applied, again modeled after the early church. All believers were equal. Some communities followed the communism in goods described in the second chapter of the Acts of the Apostles. Each believer was both priest to his fellow believer and missionary to the unbeliever (the missionary zeal of the early Anabaptists was remarkable). Each church elected its own pastor or minister. In fact, the most important symbolic moment in the early development of Anabaptism was the scene on Easter 1525 at the little town of Waldshut in southern Germany, when Balthasar Hübmaier resigned as Catholic priest and was immediately elected minister by his congregation. The congregational principle of church organization here dramatized for the first time was to have an enormously important future. The idea of separation of church and state—"a free church in a free state"—germinated among the left-wing religious groups of the early sixteenth century. It was the Anabaptists, not the leading Protestant reformers, who first caught the vision of thoroughgoing religious freedom—the right of religious groups to associate voluntarily, to elect a minister, to maintain standards of admission and continuing membership, all without interference from the state.

The social background of Anabaptism was fairly homogeneous. Although middle-class intellectuals played an important part in the movement, the radical sects drew most of their membership from the lower classes—peasants, craftsmen, weavers, miners—particularly those who were hard hit by the economic changes and social dislocations of the age. Members of the upper classes were quick to notice the apparent connection between social discontent and religious heresy. The weaving town of Zwickau in southern Saxony, for instance, already a hotbed of Waldensian heresy, was one of the earliest centers of Anabaptist agitation (1521). Zurich, Basel, Strasbourg, Nuremberg, and Augsburg, industrial cities which went over to Lutheran or Zwinglian ideas at an early stage, were also centers of radical activity at one time or another. In fact, it was the official Protestant churches—Lutheran, Zwinglian, and Calvinist—not the Roman Church, which had the most difficult time dealing with Anabaptism. Luther and Calvin cannot be understood unless one remembers that they were fighting a two-front war of ideas from the very beginning against Romanism on the right and Anabaptism on the left. If Luther and Calvin in the end preserved a great deal of mediaeval Christianity, it was because of the fear of social and religious revolution from below, which they felt perhaps even more keenly than their Catholic opponents because of the widespread accusation that they themselves were really responsible for starting the revolutionary process.

The radical sects were persecuted and martyred with a hysterical persistence which is hard at first sight to explain. The great majority of those called Anabaptists were sober, hard-working, pious people, with strong leanings toward pacifism and quietism. Most of them had little if any education. Most of them were poor, many of them embittered by social and economic oppression. The impact upon such people of direct contact with the Bible in the vernacular, either through reading or preaching, was strange and unpredictable. The conviction grew rapidly among such people that the end of the world was at hand, that God was about to usher in the millennium or thousand-year rule of the saints predicted in Revelation 20, and that they, not the Catholics or Lutherans, were God's people, the instruments of His mysterious will. To most of them it was through the suffering and martyrdom of His chosen flock that God would bring history to a close. "Suffering is the way, the door, and the means to God, the door into the sheep-stall." "A Christian without suffering is like an untrained doctor, like a house whose beam has not been hewn." A few believed that God meant to use them as human instruments of his wrath in the final struggle with evil. These few rejected suffering in favor of violence. How many there were of this kind we shall never know, but there were enough to send a thrill of terror through the ruling classes and fan the flames of persecution.

Two events in particular shaped the fate of Anabaptism and marked the chronological limits of what might be called the Anabaptist movement: the Peasants' War of 1524–1525 and the rising at Münster in 1534–1535. Anabaptist groups were beginning to appear in Switzerland and southern Germany when the Peasants' War broke out in these same districts. The causes of this greatest of sixteenth-century lower-class uprisings had relatively little to do with religion. They lay deep in the stresses and strains produced in feudalism and the old manorial system by the new economic forces. But one of the most prominent of the rebels' demands was that each community be given the right to choose its own pastor, and some Anabaptist leaders were involved. The rebellion was a bloody business, and its suppression even more bloody. Luther was at first convinced that blame for the rising was about equally divided between the nobility and the peasantry, but as the violence increased, he turned on the rebels with bitter vituperation.

The net result of the war was a decade of upper-class panic and social repression which had its repercussions in religion as well as politics. In the late 1520's savage laws for the punishment of Anabaptists were revived or instituted all over Europe and a reign of terror began in which hundreds of religious radicals of all kinds were tortured, burned, drowned, or put to the sword. Although permanently stamped out in most of Germany, groups of survivors fled to Moravia, Poland, the lower Rhine Valley, and the Netherlands, whence they eventually had their influence on England and America. In 1534–1535 the city of Münster became by chance a haven for Anabaptists of the more wild-eyed variety, who set up a sort of military communistic regime which lasted about a year. The radicals were finally defeated and slaughtered by an army raised with the co-operation of both Lutherans and Catholics. Violence was now finally

discredited, and the Anabaptists under Menno Simons'
leadership (Mennonites) turned unanimously to the way
of suffering, the way that had always been that of the
majority.

In attempting to describe the essence of Anabaptism, we
have inevitably made the whole left wing of the Reformation
seem more homogeneous than it really was. Roland H.
Bainton, the leading American student of the subject, points
out that the left wing included a bewildering variety of
sects and individuals with a baffling variety of beliefs, often
incompatible. They ranged all the way from individualistic
mystics and rationalistic Unitarians to evangelical pietists,
Biblical literalists, and fanatical millennialists. These were
people "distraught by persecution and wrought up to a
temperature at which incompatibles fuse on an emotional
rather than a logical level," Bainton writes; "A thermometer
is more appropriate than a ruler for measuring such theolo-
gies." [3] Nevertheless, despite this variety, there is no denying
the importance for the later history of both church and
state of the leading ideas on which nearly all Anabaptists
agreed: restitution of primitive Christianity, the church as
a voluntary association of believers, and separation of church
and state.

The Case of England

"The one definite thing which can be said about the
Reformation in England," writes Sir Maurice Powicke, "is
that it was an act of State." [4] The ecclesiastical revolution

[3] R. H. Bainton, "The Left Wing of the Reformation," *Journal
of Religion*, XXI (April 1941), 131.

[4] *The Reformation in England* (London: Oxford University
Press, 1941), p. 1.

which took place in England during the reign of Henry VIII (1509–1547) has been traditionally difficult to describe because it arose unexpectedly out of a seemingly trivial personal matter, because the juridical breach with the papacy preceded rather than followed doctrinal difference, and because there has always been wide disagreement about the proper interpretation of what happened. English historians would have us believe that the case of England was unique, but if there were peculiar elements in the English Reformation, there were many other elements which had strong parallels elsewhere.

In a sense, the adoption of Lutheranism on the continent, whether in a free city like Augsburg, an electorate like Brandenburg, or a monarchy like Sweden, was always "an act of state." Acts of legislation by the municipal council or by the prince and his estates were always the decisive event, although preaching, disputation, and popular agitation were the usual preludes to political action. Throughout Europe, Protestantism failed to take root and grow wherever it was unable to capture the state or at least to stake out some territorial or legal basis for minority existence (as in France). In this sense there was nothing unique about the English developments. But England was the largest and most important political unit to secede at one blow from Catholic Christendom. The intricate relationship between political and religious factors in the process may be studied in England, therefore, on a relatively large scale. This is worth doing for the further reason that the accession of England to the Protestant cause was in a sense decisive. If England had remained Catholic, it seems fairly certain that Protestantism later on could not have maintained itself in the Netherlands, and it is at least arguable that in this case all

of Europe except for a few innocuous Lutheran states in
Germany might have been won back to Roman Christianity
by the end of the century.

Henry VIII's desire to gain an annulment of his marriage
to Catherine of Aragon because he needed a male heir to
the throne and because he wanted to marry Anne Boleyn
was the direct cause of England's breach with the papal
jurisdiction. In 1527 Catherine was past childbearing; the
lack of a male heir might throw England into a new War
of the Roses; and the king was infatuated with Anne. Catherine was the emperor Charles V's aunt, and Pope Clement
VII was under the emperor's thumb. It was not surprising,
therefore—although it was exasperating to Henry—that the
pope should deny the king's desire. When tact and persuasion failed, Henry resorted to threats. Wolsey failed to get
his monarch what he wanted, was cast down from power,
and died. The new royal secretary, Thomas Cromwell, was
more unscrupulous if less showy. Together he and the king
worked to mobilize the whole nation in Henry's support in
order to threaten the pope with secession from papal jurisdiction unless the annulment were granted. Parliament was
summoned in 1529. In 1531 the English clergy assembled
in Convocation were frightened into acknowledging that
Henry was "Supreme Head of the Church in England," and
next year they gave up their right to make laws for the
church in Convocation apart from king and Parliament. In
the spring of 1533 Anne was pregnant and the pace was
quickened. Threats gave way to acts. Parliament passed a
statute cutting off appeals from English ecclesiastical courts
to Rome, and the new archbishop of Canterbury, Thomas
Cranmer, straightway held court and granted Henry his
annulment, enabling him to make Anne his queen. In 1534

a series of acts of Parliament finally stopped all financial payments and judicial appeals to Rome, declared that "the King's Majesty justly and rightfully is and ought to be . . . the only Supreme Head in earth of the Church of England," and fixed the succession to the throne upon the children of Henry and Anne (their only child Elizabeth was born in September 1533). Within the next few years some 550 English monasteries were dissolved, their property confiscated by the crown, and their 7,000 inmates pensioned and thrust out into secular life. Henry had cut England off from obedience to the pope.

All this amounted to a revolution. In mediaeval England, as in the rest of Christendom, church and state had been considered co-ordinate and complementary authorities, no matter how confusing the conflicts and compromises between the two powers might be. Spiritual jurisdiction had belonged to the pope and the clergy, temporal jurisdiction to the king and his representatives. It was hard to draw the line in practice, but in theory there was a clear sharp difference between the two powers. Now the king was "Supreme Head of the Church of England." What did this mean? Had the state absorbed the church? Had Henry stepped into the pope's shoes so far as one nation was concerned (without of course claiming the power of a priest to administer the sacraments)? The answer was a tentative yes, but no clear answer ever was given. The closest approach was the famous preamble to the Act in Restraint of Appeals of 1533, which argued that

By divers sundry old authentic histories and chronicles it is manifestly declared and expressed that this realm of England is an empire [that is, subject to no higher authority] . . . governed by one Supreme Head and King . . . unto whom a body politic, compact of all sorts and degrees of people divided in terms and by names of Spiritualty and Temporalty, be bounden and owe to bear next to God a natural and humble obedience; he being also institute and furnished by the goodness and sufferance of Almighty God with plenary, whole, and entire power . . . without restraint or provocation [appeal] to any foreign princes or potentates of the world.

This was the theory then: Whatever other nations in Christendom might be, England was a sovereign territorial state subject to a single monarch; within this state clergy and laity alike were subjects owing obedience to the king; no foreign prince, including the bishop of Rome, had any jurisdiction whatever in England. And yet this theory left all the important questions really unanswered. What then is the "Catholic Church"? Where is the ultimate authority in the church? Did this mean that England had automatically joined the Lutheran fold? Henry insisted not. In doctrine and liturgy, the Church of England still belonged to the Catholic Church, and an "Act abolishing diversity of opinions" was put through Parliament in 1539 to stress this fact by reaffirming the Real Presence of Christ in the Eucharist and several other points of orthodox belief. But a significant phrase in the Act of Supremacy of 1534, repeated in other Tudor legislation, gave the king "full power and authority from time to time to visit, repress, redress, reform, order, correct, restrain, and amend all . . . errors, heresies, abuses, offences, contempts, and enormities, whatsoever they be," in the English Church. In effect, this was the most spectacular response to Luther's appeal of 1520 to the ruling powers of the secular order to take in hand the matter of ecclesiastical reform since the clergy had failed to reform themselves. It is not far wrong to say that what happened in England during the reign of Henry VIII was the establishment of the legal supremacy of the state over the church.

The revolution was accomplished with relatively little bloodshed, the matchless martyrdom of Sir Thomas More (1535) being the best known of the executions. There were several reasons for this. Englishmen and their king had vivid memories of the violence and anarchy of the Wars of the Roses and wanted no repetition of civil war. Henry moved cautiously and with ostentatious respect for legality. Most people sympathized warmly with Catherine as a much put-upon woman, but Henry dragged the red herrings of national patriotism and anticlerical feeling across the trail of his intentions so skillfully that he was able to direct the animosity of people and Parliament against the pope and the clergy at every crucial point of the negotiations. No significant changes were made in the church services which the ordinary Englishman attended, so no real consciousness of revolution reached him. Furthermore, the actual issues were always confused and, as always in revolutions, even the leaders could not see clearly where they were going. The net result was that Englishmen generally accepted the breach with Rome without effective protest, although there is no evidence that the majority wanted it.

Sir Thomas More, on trial for his life against a trumped-up charge of treason to his king, saw to the heart of the issue in a way that almost no other did:

Therefore am I not bounden, my Lord, to conform my conscience to the Council of one realm against the general Council of Christendom. For of the foresaid holy bishops I have, for every bishop of yours [who backed the king], above one hundred; and for one Council or Parliament of yours (God knoweth what manner of one), I have all the Councils made these thousand years. And for this one kingdom, I have all other Christian realms.[5]

Luther's conscience supported the individual against the Catholic Church. More's conscience supported the universal church against the national state.

By the time of Henry VIII's death it was clear that England was committed to moving in a certain direction and could not stand still as the aging king might have wished. Henry had unleashed the dangerously powerful new force of national sentiment to gain his way with the pope. He had held the line on doctrine, but he had consented to having English Bibles set up in all the churches. Men were reading the Scriptures and what came out of Wittenberg and Zurich and Strasbourg. There was a Protestant party led by the archbishop Cranmer. It was a tiny minority, but it was a determined and intelligent minority. England in 1547 was headed in the direction of more intense patriotism and more extreme Protestantism.

The Sovereignty of God

Luther was a religious leader of marvelous sensitivity to universal human needs, but he was not the sort of person to give the movement he initiated a systematic theology and a disciplined ecclesiastical organization. The second generation of Protestant reformers sensed the need for these things, and it was John Calvin (1509–1564), above all, and the church which he inspired at Geneva, which supplied them. Calvin was the theologian and organizer of the Protestant movement.

Industrious scholars have demonstrated that Calvin never

[5] Nicholas Harpsfield, *The Life and Death of Sir Thomas Moore,* ed. Elsie V. Hitchcock (London, 1932), p. 196.

had a truly original idea in his life; his leading ideas of doctrine and church organization can all be traced to Luther, Bucer, Augustine or other Fathers, or the Bible itself. But the result was a creative achievement nevertheless. "Calvinism" was a distinct form of Protestant Christianity with a characteristic flavor to its theology, its ethics, and its social organization. Furthermore, it became the militant, international form of Protestantism, imbued with a sense of its own destiny to conquer men's souls and usher in the Kingdom of God. In the form of "Puritanism" it left a deep mark on both British and American civilization.

Calvin shared with Luther the four central Protestant beliefs already described (p. 53). But he was born a generation after Luther in a different land, he was a far different sort of person, and his education and career were significantly different. He was a Frenchman, educated as a Humanist and a lawyer. To this education he seems to have owed his fine style both in Latin and French, his interest in ethical problems, and his legal cast of mind. Converted to Protestant beliefs about 1533, he meant to follow a career of scholarship and writing, but on a chance visit to Geneva in 1536 the local Protestant leader, William Farel, called down a "frightful imprecation" upon him if he refused to set aside his scholarly plans and help the cause of the Gospel in Geneva. Unwillingly Calvin stayed, and except for three years of exile during which he visited Bucer in Strasbourg (1538–1541), he remained in Geneva as the city's leading minister and unofficial "city manager" until his death.

The contrast with Luther was striking. It appears in the portraits of the two men. As Luther grew older his face and figure filled out, and a kind of confidence and reconciliation with himself is suggested in the lines of eyes and mouth.

As Calvin grew older he became even thinner than he was as a young man, and the perpendicular lines of his long nose and firm, thin lips suggest the increasingly flintlike qualities of his mind and personality. He demanded much of himself and of others. He had great organizing and executive ability. He could inspire passionate devotion in his followers—and equally passionate hatred in his enemies. Luther was a peasant, a monk, and a university professor; Calvin, a scholar and lawyer called to a turbulent public ministry in a flourishing business community. Naturally they were impressed by different needs and emphasized different Christian solutions. The foundations were the same, but the structures of doctrine and practice erected at Wittenberg and Geneva were different in many important respects.

Calvin's two most characteristic achievements were his great manual of Protestant theology, *Institutes of the Christian Religion* (first edition 1536, final edition 1559), and the well-organized and tightly disciplined church which he set up in Geneva after 1541. In the first, he played the part in Protestant history which Thomas Aquinas had played for mediaeval Catholicism in summarizing and systematizing doctrine. In the second, he played the part taken in Catholic history by Innocent III and the other great mediaeval popes. Rarely are theoretical and practical abilities combined in one man as they were in Calvin. His *Institutes* went through edition after edition in almost every major European language and influenced the thought of generations of Protestants in Europe and America. The Genevan church was the model for organizing what were called "the Reformed churches" of France, the Netherlands, Scotland, parts of Germany, Poland, Bohemia, and Hungary. From the 1540's and 1550's on, it was to Geneva that young Protestant enthusiasts went from all over Europe to see what John Knox called "the most perfect school of Christ that ever was on earth since the days of the apostles." It was there that they received the theological training and the ideas of church and state which they carried back home to put into practice. And it was from Geneva that Calvin himself kept in touch with many of them in a voluminous correspondence. To his followers, Geneva seemed to be the beachhead established by God from which the victory of the Kingdom would some day be organized. To Roman Catholics, Geneva was the center of a satanic international conspiracy, subversive of all government and religion.

Calvin's central belief around which all else revolved was the absolute sovereignty of God. "God asserts His possession of omnipotence," he wrote, "and claims our acknowledgment of this attribute; not such as is imagined by sophists, vain, idle, and almost asleep, but vigilant, efficacious, operative, and engaged in continual action." God is "the Arbiter and Governor of all things, who, in His own wisdom, has, from the remotest eternity, decreed what He would do, and now, by His own power, executes what He has decreed." It follows that He "has once and for all determined, both whom He would admit to salvation, and whom He would condemn to destruction." If this seems unjust by human standards, we must remember that "the will of God is the highest rule of justice, so that what He wills must be considered just, for this very reason, because He wills it." [6]

The sovereignty of God with its corollary of predestination had been implicit in Luther's conviction that in the process of salvation God does everything, man nothing.

[6] *Institutes* I, 16, 3; I, 16, 8; III, 21, 7; III, 23, 2. Tr. by John Allen (Philadelphia, 1930).

Luther had insisted upon this principle in arguing against Erasmus' Humanistic belief in man's power at least to co-operate with God, and Bucer had worked the principle out still further. After his visit with Bucer, Calvin made the sovereignty of God the main theme of his *Institutes*. It had several important corollaries.

The first was that if only God is sovereign, then no man —whether he be pope or king—has any claim to absolute power. Certainly the Church of Rome has no such claim. Nor in the last analysis has any secular government. Calvin was very careful not to preach what we would call the "right of revolution"; the burden of his teaching was obedience to legally constituted governments. But he dropped one very fruitful hint at the close of the *Institutes* which was developed by his followers, particularly where they were a religious minority (as they were almost everywhere), into the doctrine of constitutional resistance to tyranny. This was the hint that in countries which have representative assemblies it is the right and duty of these assemblies to resist the wrongful doings of monarchs. Calvinist minorities in France, Scotland, and the Netherlands were to insist, as John Knox did before Mary Queen of Scots, that "right religion takes neither original [origin] nor authority from worldly princes but from the eternal God alone, so are not subjects bound to frame their religion according to the appetite of their princes." Peter's reply to the Sanhedrin (Acts 5:29)—"One must obey God rather than men"—was a favorite text with these stubborn, high-minded followers of Calvin who put the sovereignty of God before the sovereignty of man. One of the key factors in the development of modern constitutional government was the resistance of

Calvinist minorities to the exercise of arbitrary power by monarchs.

Another corollary was that this busy, active, sovereign God uses His elect for a purpose: to witness to His glory and to usher in His Kingdom. Good works cannot save a man, but God does good works *through* men. The whole world is "the theatre of God's glory." He is working out his majestic and inscrutable purpose in His church, advancing its cause, overthrowing its enemies, purifying its members. The ethic of Calvinists, therefore, was dynamic, activistic, and, above all, social. Calvin's writings are filled with military terminology. God's people are an army on the march, the battle is hot and nearing its climax. There is no sure sign in this world of who belongs to the army of the elect and who does not, but it does no good to worry about one's salvation since all is predestined. What counts is the sense of being used by God to carry out His historical purpose—as Calvin was sure God had used him by snatching him from the scholar's cloister to do battle against the enemies of the Gospel in Geneva. The sovereignty of God meant that God was always working through men and through history. The danger was that it was so easy for Calvin's followers to become convinced that they were God's elect and the sole instruments of His will.

A final corollary was that God reveals His sovereignty through His Word and exercises it directly through His church. To Luther, God's Word was contained *in* the Bible, but to Calvin the Word *was* the Bible, all of it. The Bible then was a Christian's first and last authority. God has revealed in it everything necessary, and nothing unnecessary, for man to know about his salvation. The Bible is the foundation of the church, not the church of the Bible as Romanists maintained. But the church nevertheless has a very important function to fulfill. The church is a divine institution in which the Word is properly preached and the sacraments rightly administered. It is in no way subject to the secular government except in obviously secular matters, and it has the duty of guiding the secular power in spiritual matters. It has therefore a real autonomy and initiative as a social institution, in conformity with the principle that God alone is its sovereign. In all the Calvinist churches the principle of congregational election was maintained in choosing the four orders of ministers, teachers, elders, and deacons, and this principle blended easily with Anabaptist principles in the seventeenth century to produce a genuine democracy in English left-wing churches, a practice which was an important root of modern democracy. But in practice the Calvinist clergy exercised a strong control over their congregations in matters of right belief and conduct. The Reformed Churches operated on the principle of according the laity an important share in church government but reserving initiative and leadership to the clergy.

It may already have struck the reader that what Calvin set himself to build was a kind of non-Roman Catholicism. Calvin was bitterly antipapal, but he was also deeply fearful of the threat of anarchy from the Anabaptists on the left. As a result he saw the importance of discipline and organization, of authority and historical continuity, more clearly than Luther. He denied none of Luther's basic beliefs, but the shape he gave to Protestant theology and church organization is in some ways more reminiscent of the scholasticism and ecclesiastical supremacy of the thirteenth century than it is of Lutheranism, Anglicanism, or Anabaptism.

Calvin's international Reformed Church with its "colloquies" and "synods," in France, the Netherlands, Scotland, and elsewhere, independent of the state, guided by a devout and educated clergy, claiming to influence and shape the whole of life, thinking of itself as a militant army of God—all this was very like the church of the Crusades and the Schoolmen. And yet at the same time the Reformed churches were thoroughly Protestant. They had no head on earth—however much his enemies might joke about Calvin as the Protestant pope. The laity never allowed the Calvinist ministry to regain the position of the Catholic priesthood. And the Calvinist churches never succeeded in subordinating secular governments to theocratic control except for a short time in Geneva and New England. Calvinism belonged unmistakably to Protestantism, but it paradoxically preserved many lines of continuity with mediaeval Christianity.

The year 1559 may be taken to mark the coming of age of Calvinism. In that year Calvin published the definitive edition of the *Institutes* and founded the University of Geneva. During the same year the first national synod of Reformed Churches met in France, Calvinism was taking deep root in the Netherlands and central Europe, and ministers trained in Geneva were hurrying back to England from their exile on the continent during Mary's reign. In the following year, John Knox worked a Calvinist revolution in Scotland. Militant Protestantism seemed to be irresistibly on the march.

The Catholic Reformation

The religious upheaval of the sixteenth century included two major movements: a Protestant Reformation, which because of its newness and complexity we have described at some length, and a Catholic Reformation. The latter has sometimes been interpreted as a Catholic counterattack against Protestantism, sometimes as an indigenous revival of Catholic piety having nothing to do with Protestantism. The truth is that what happened in the Catholic half of western Christendom was both a Counter Reformation (as Protestant historians tend to call it) and a Catholic Reformation (as Catholic historians describe it). Its roots were fed by forces originating far before Luther's time, but the form it took was largely determined by the Protestant attack.

The Catholic Reformation consisted of two closely related developments: first, a revival of Christian piety among the secular and regular clergy and to some extent among the laity, rooted in the monastic tradition, in mysticism, and in Christian Humanism; and second, a series of institutional reforms including administrative changes, doctrinal definition, and coercive measures, which were inspired to some extent by the revival of piety, but to a larger extent by the need of countering Protestant heresy and schism. Faced by the defection of almost half Europe, the Catholic Church developed spiritual resources which hardly seemed to exist when Luther first appeared on the scene, strengthened its organization, and rolled back the tide of heresy until by the end of the century Protestantism was limited roughly to the northern third of Europe, as it is today.

The sixteenth century produced a remarkable variety of Catholic saints: the English lawyer and statesman, Thomas More; the cheerful and imaginative Savoyard, François de Sales; the somber reforming archbishop of Milan, Charles Borromeo; the whimsical Florentine, Philip Neri; the rapturous Spanish mystic, Teresa; and most influential of all, the founder of the Jesuit Order, Ignatius Loyola. The Catholic revival began from within, in the spiritual struggles of monks and priests, occasionally of laymen. Older monastic orders were reformed and new orders were founded, particularly in Italy. Before Luther posted his theses, a distinguished and aristocratic group of Christian Humanists and others at Rome had formed a pious brotherhood called the Oratory of Divine Love. Their guiding belief was that the reformation of church and society begins in the individual soul. Never large in numbers, the Oratory had enormous indirect influence, stimulating the reform of older monastic orders and of the secular clergy, and contributing leaders to the Council of Trent. But it was Spain even more than Italy which was to be the radiating center of renewed Catholic zeal. Spanish patriotism and Spanish Christianity had been fused and tempered in the long struggle with the Moslems. In a society disturbed by the presence in its midst of half-converted Jews and Moors, Catholic orthodoxy was considered the bulwark of social order. The work of the Spanish Inquisition was popular, even if its methods were dreaded. Spain was the nerve center of the Catholic Reformation.

About ten years after Luther underwent his conversion experience in Wittenberg, a romantic young Basque soldier who had had his leg permanently crippled by a cannon ball underwent conversion of a somewhat different sort at Manresa in Spain (1522). The soldier was Ignatius Loyola, and his spiritual experience resulted in the founding of the Society of Jesus, or Jesuits. Luther came out of his spiritual struggle convinced that man's sinfulness is inherent, that he cannot save himself, and that only a merciful God can save him. Loyola came out of his struggle believing that both God and Satan are external to man, that man has the power to choose between them, and that by the disciplined use of his imagination—vividly picturing to himself, for instance, the horrors of hell and the sufferings of Christ—he can so strengthen his will as to make the choice for God. Where Luther and Protestantism ended in a belief in predestination and the utter sovereignty of God, Loyola and the Catholic Church insisted upon man's free will and his power to co-operate with God—even, according to Loyola, to the point of influencing the course of the battle between the armies of God and of Satan by his choice. Luther denied man's free will; Loyola glorified it and set out to discipline it by the use of imagination. The record of his method, *Spiritual Exercises*, was one of the most influential books of the century.

The Society of Jesus, which Loyola founded and which the pope approved in 1540, bore the stamp of its founder's personality in its every rule. The aim of the order was simple and unoriginal: to restore the Roman Catholic Church to the position of spiritual power and temporal influence which it had held three centuries before. It was the methods which were relatively new. Their keynote was a thoroughly modern idea: efficiency. Everything was to be subordinated to the major aim of bringing all men within the fold of the church. The Society or Company of Jesus was to be fashioned into an efficient fighting weapon, absolutely obedient to the pope and ready to believe that "what seems black is white if the hierarchical church so teaches." The *Constitutions* of the order are even more saturated in military terminology than Calvin's writings. The Jesuit was to wear no distinctive habit but to dress as his particular job of priest, teacher, or missionary might demand. He was not to exhaust himself by ascetic practices but to remember that tangible results in the service of the church are what count.

He was not to trouble sensitive consciences in the confessional, but to remind the sinner that only acts of deliberate will are truly sinful and so encourage him not to lose heart. "Send no one away dejected," wrote Loyola. "God asks nothing impossible," he believed—and his followers were the great apostles of the possible. They saw the importance of influencing young minds, and their schools and universities were models of rational planning and discipline, the envy of Protestants. They saw the advantage of winning the key persons in society, and so became confessors to the great. Their missions to India and China gained spectacular results in conversions, partly by not demanding too much of the convert. In central Europe they were the shock troops of Catholic counterattack against Protestantism, and by the end of the century Poland, Bohemia, Hungary, and south Germany—which had all seemed on the verge of going Protestant—were safely back in the Catholic camp with only Protestant minorities within their borders. The Jesuits were the hard core of the Catholic Reformation, illustrating nicely the intimate connection between spiritual revival and shrewd adaptation of means to ends in the cause of "counter reformation."

Individual saints and even devoted monastic orders could hardly accomplish much unless means were found to reform the whole clerical hierarchy from the pope down to the parish clergy. The two traditional approaches to this problem were either to demand that the papacy reform itself or that a general council of the whole church be summoned to do the job. Both approaches were tried in the sixteenth century, with some success in each. Beginning with Paul III (1534–1549), men of more conscience and moral responsibility began to be elected to the papacy, and they in turn

appointed abler cardinals. Abuses were not reformed overnight, but after mid-century the popes were generally
capable and vigorous men, and sometimes zealous reformers
like Pius V (1566–1572). The College of Cardinals, organized at the end of the century into standing committees
called congregations, was an integral part of the reformed
papacy.

The Council of Trent, held in three separate sessions
(1545–1547, 1551–1552, 1562–1563), was the focal point of
all the reforming efforts within the church. There were
so many conflicting views of what a general council might
accomplish that it is a wonder any was summoned at all.
The emperor Charles V was the strongest supporter of a
council, hoping that the Protestants would attend (which
they never did) and that the religious schism would be
healed. King Francis I of France was not enthusiastic about
a council unless he could dominate it. Many bishops
throughout Europe hoped that a council would increase
their local authority and their independence of the papacy.
The popes were generally afraid of summoning a council
for fear that it would fall under the control of an alliance
between the bishops and the secular rulers, who would
whittle down the papal power and perhaps compromise
with Protestantism.

The result was a papal triumph. In spite of the difficulties,
a general council met at Trent. From the beginning the
popes managed to exclude the influence of lay rulers from
the Council's important decisions and to dominate the vot-
ing by seeing that there was always a working majority of
Italian prelates and (in the later sessions) a shock force
of Jesuits to guide discussion. Dogmatic definition and administrative reforms were taken up in alternate sittings. The

major tenets of mediaeval Catholic belief which had been challenged by Protestantism were now for the first time sharply defined and made dogma: salvation was not by faith alone, but by faith and works combined; authority lay not in the Bible alone, but in the Latin Vulgate translation of the Bible as interpreted by the church, and in the traditions which were preserved in the church. The authority of the bishops within their dioceses was somewhat expanded, but they were more explicitly subjected to papal control. Moral reforms were agreed upon and provision made for establishing seminaries for the training of priests in every diocese. A creed binding upon the clergy was drawn up, and the sacraments were redefined.

The upshot was that the Catholic Church closed its ranks, formulated its fundamental dogma in opposition to Protestantism, provided for some, though by no means all, the moral and administrative reform demanded by various parties, and thus saved over half of Europe for Roman Catholicism. All this was not accomplished without coercion. The mediaeval Inquisition was revived in somewhat different forms in Spain (1480), the Netherlands (1523), and Italy (1542). A Roman Index of prohibited books was drawn up in 1559, to be followed by another authorized by the Council of Trent and afterward kept up to date by a "Congregation of the Index" in the College of Cardinals. But the essential fact was that in the face of Protestant appeals to the secular power to reform the church and of Catholic monarchs' attempts to set up national churches, the Roman Church had reasserted its spiritual independence. It had strengthened its own internal organization and had regained much if not all of the moral prestige it had lost during the later Middle Ages. Critics accused the Fathers at Trent of stifling further intellectual growth in the church by putting believers in dogmatic strait jackets. And enemies of the Jesuits accused them of fatal compromises with worldly methods and of "putting cushions under sinners' elbows." But the achievement was considerable. Granting the irrevocable loss of Protestant lands and peoples, the Church of Rome was far stronger and better able to face the future in 1600 than it had been in 1500.

The Religious Balance Sheet

It is not easy to sum up the historical significance of the religious upheaval in a few words. We see now that the religious unity of western Christendom was permanently shattered, but the full significance of this fact was not borne in upon Europeans all at once. At first Luther's followers thought him so obviously right that the Catholic Church would inevitably adopt his ideas. Others thought him so obviously a heretic that sooner or later he would be burned and his movement wither away. After all, the papal schism of the fourteenth century had finally been healed, and one heretical movement after another in the history of the church had either been wiped out or walled off and rendered innocuous. None of the Protestant leaders of the first and second generations thought they were breaking from the true, universal, catholic Church of Christ, but only from a false Roman version of it. Until the conference of 1541 between Protestants and Catholics at Ratisbon, reunion always seemed a possibility.

As time went on, however, a second stage was imperceptibly reached in the thinking of ordinary men. The uneasy, half-conscious conviction grew that a stalemate had been reached. Catholicism could not crush out the new heresy,

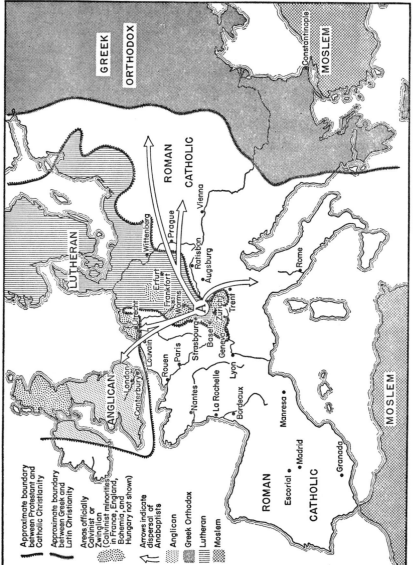

Religious divisions of Europe about 1600

and Protestantism could not win over Rome. In this second stage, there was as yet no real emotional or intellectual acceptance of the fact of stalemate, only bitter admission that it was so. The vast majority of men were still convinced that religious truth was one. Truth stood on one side, error on the other. Error meant not only individual damnation, but infection of others and social subversion. Naturally the corollary was coercion—inquisition and persecution, civil war and international war. At this stage the coercion was perhaps even more bitter because of the haunting suspicion in some minds that it might not prove effective. Almost no one could yet attain the view that in two contending religious systems, there might be some truth on both sides, and that if only enough men could see this, the two systems might peacefully coexist on the same continent and even in the same state. The spirit of the mid-sixteenth century is exactly expressed by the inquisitor who remarked, "It is no great matter whether they that die on account of religion be guilty or innocent, provided we terrify the people by such examples." [7]

The third stage of religious toleration resulting from full acceptance of the fact of religious pluralism and diversity was only hinted at before 1600 in the attitudes of mystics, Christian Humanists like Erasmus, radical Protestants like Sebastian Castellio (whom Calvin hounded out of Geneva), skeptics like Michel de Montaigne, and practical politicians like Queen Elizabeth of England and King Henry IV of France.

One thing seems clear. The Protestant and Catholic Reformations temporarily halted the underlying trend toward

[7] Quoted by R. H. Bainton, *The Reformation of the Sixteenth Century* (Boston: Beacon Press, 1952), p. 224.

secularization in European society. Even granting the obvious secular tendencies in both Calvinist and Jesuit ethics, for example, it remains true that sixteenth-century Europe was more troubled by religious concerns than fifteenth-century Europe. Luther "revived the Christian consciousness of Europe," Roland Bainton writes; "religion became again a dominant factor even in politics for another century and a half. Men cared enough for the faith to die for it and to kill for it. If there is any sense remaining of Christian civilization in the West, this man Luther in no small measure deserves the credit." [8]

In more concrete terms, this meant that at the height of "the Renaissance"—the moment in European history when the church's prestige seemed near extinction, the secular national state irresistibly on the rise, and social life in general becoming more and more permeated by secular ideals—Christian ideals and institutions acquired a new autonomy and dynamism. The state churches of Germany and England of the 1530's were not the final solution. By mid-century the Calvinists and the Jesuits were setting the pace, each representing a sort of supranational religious ideology embodied in a militant organization, proselytizing across national boundaries, and calling for an allegiance transcending every secular political tie. The clash of these new militant religious ideologies with the already deep-rooted dynastic and national loyalties gave the struggle for power of the later sixteenth century its peculiar character and intensity.

[8] *Here I Stand* (New York and Nashville: Abingdon-Cokesbury [now Abingdon Press], 1950), pp. 21–22.

CHAPTER III

The Struggle for Power

THE latter half of the sixteenth century witnessed a sharp struggle for power resulting from the convergence of forces liberated by the religious upheavals of the preceding period.

Europe's economy was subjected to severe strain by the spectacular rise in prices which began about the middle of the century. The war expenditures and devaluation policies of European governments had something to do with the inflationary movement, but the main cause was the mounting flood of precious metal which poured into Europe from Spanish America after the opening of the fabulously rich silver mines at Potosí in Peru (1545). The influx of bullion far surpassed the normal need of a growing economy for an expanding medium of exchange and so pushed prices skyward, first in Spain and then in the rest of Europe. As always, inflation led to social stress, hurting the classes which like the older nobility depended upon fairly fixed incomes and favoring the entrepreneur and speculator. A "new nobility" began to appear in England and France, consisting of members of the bourgeoisie or the gentry who were able to climb to titles of nobility amid the economic or political ruin of older feudal families.

Religious animosities added to the general tension. Europe was becoming a continent of exiles and displaced persons. The political exile had been a familiar figure in Italy since the party struggles of Dante's day. Now in Europe at large the refugee from an unsuccessful political revolt was joined by the religious outcast, and many towns were coming to accept as familiar figures the exiled Jew or Catholic, the fugitive Lutheran or Calvinist or Anabaptist.

Finally, the economic, social, and religious tensions were reflected in and aggravated by political tensions. The relatively simple dynastic war between Hapsburgs and Valois (1522–1559) gave place in the latter part of the century to a series of struggles which were partly international, partly civil wars. In these struggles religion sometimes reinforced patriotism but just as often undermined it. The wars and rebellions reflected the general economic and social instability as well as the new intransigence of religious groups (like the Calvinists and Jesuits). Governments struggled against bankruptcy with varying degrees of success. Ruined nobles and rising merchants often became warmongers, for different reasons but hoping for personal gain in the result. Embittered religious exiles urged governments on to more belligerent stands than they would otherwise have taken. The struggle for power which ensued was not only between states but also between churches and classes. Rebellions led to wars when traitors were supported by sympathizers or coreligionists abroad, and wars in turn induced rebellions. In the years 1568–1572, for instance, there were rebellions in Spain, France, the Netherlands, and England. In each case the rebels were more formidable because of the threat of support from friends abroad: the Moriscoes in Spain from Moslems in North Africa, the Huguenots in France from English Protestants, the Calvinists in the Netherlands from French and English sympathizers, the Catholics in the north of England from Catholic Spain. The roots of war and rebellion were never simply economic or political or religious; they were all of these. In fact, in the confusion of social, political, and ideological elements in its wars and revolutions, the later sixteenth century was not unlike the twentieth.

Mid-Century: The Crucial 50's

During the ten years or so after the deaths of Luther (1546), Henry VIII (1547), and Francis I (1547), crucial decisions were made and important events took place which were to influence the course of European history for half a century. The 1550's are the turning point of the sixteenth century.

War broke out in Germany in 1546. It was partly a religious war of Lutheran against Catholic, partly a political revolt of discontented princes against the emperor Charles V. Charles won a signal victory over the rebels at Mühlberg in 1547, but he was unable to impose the kind of peace settlement he would have liked, a broad but firm re-Catholicizing of Germany. Lutheranism was by now too deeply rooted and the independence of the princes too firmly established for that. The emperor was weary of his long years of trying to roll back the Turkish tide on the Danube and in the Mediterranean, to curb French aggression, and to limit the spread of heresy in the empire, all at the same time. The task was too much for his resources, and in 1555 he agreed to the Religious Peace of Augsburg drafted by the Imperial Diet.

The Peace of Augsburg was an unwilling recognition of religious stalemate which resulted in a certain measure of toleration. It stated simply that the emperor, princes, and states of the empire "will not make war upon any state of the empire on account of the Augsburg Confession" and the Lutheran doctrine contained in it, and that the Lutheran states would not disturb the Catholic states. This meant that each ruler or town council was now free to determine the religion of his own territory, provided it was one of the two confessions mentioned. Adherents of other religions were "altogether excluded" from the Peace —a provision which made trouble later because of the rapid growth of Calvinism in parts of Bohemia and the Rhineland. Individual Lutherans or Catholics caught in a territory of the opposite religion could "go with wife and children to another place" in the empire, and since it was usually not far to go to find a territory of their own persuasion, many left their homes to swell the army of displaced people.

Shortly before the Peace of Augsburg, Charles V seemed to have closed the iron ring about his life-long enemy France by marrying his son Philip to Queen Mary of England (1554). But the marriage was to prove barren in every respect. No heir was born, and instead of uniting England with Spain and the Netherlands in a powerful dynastic union as it was meant to do, the marriage taught Englishmen to dislike Spaniards and gained Philip nothing. In the winter of 1555–1556, Charles abdicated as ruler of the Netherlands and king of Spain in favor of Philip. He had already handed over the Hapsburg possessions in Austria to his brother Ferdinand, who was elected emperor. In 1558 Queen Mary died, and in 1559 Philip settled the latest phase of the Hapsburg wars with France and returned to Spain, never to leave the land he loved above all his other possessions until his death in 1598.

Charles's decision to leave the Netherlands to his "Spanish" son Philip rather than to his "German" brother Ferdinand was right by sixteenth-century dynastic reasoning. The money markets of the Netherlands were economically necessary to Spain, and England might yet be permanently swung into the Hapsburg orbit. But in the end the decision proved to be short-sighted. In splitting the Hapsburg empire into an Austrian and Spanish half, Charles was blind to the fact that the Netherlands belonged more naturally with the German states on grounds of religion and culture than with distant Spain. It was a fateful decision for both the Netherlands and Spain.

In France equally decisive events were taking place in the decade after Francis I's death. During the reign of Henry II (1547–1559) Calvinism grew and spread in France, in spite of the vigorous efforts of the government to prevent it. More by force of circumstances than by conscious design, the French government turned its main attention from Italy, where French armies had been involved off and on since 1494, to the northeastern frontier, taking important territory near the Rhine and expelling the English from their last continental foothold, Calais. This left Spain in control of Italy and inaugurated the long French attempts, undertaken in earnest during the next century, to expand toward the Netherlands and the Rhineland. Apparently all was well with France when peace was made with Philip of Spain in 1559. The monarchy appeared to be strong and growing stronger at home and abroad. But in July 1559 Henry II died of wounds received in a tournament, leaving three weakling sons all under age, and his shrewd but unpopular widow, the Italian Catherine de' Medici, as regent.

All the centrifugal forces, religious and political, which had hitherto been held in check by a strong monarchy now broke loose, and France found herself in the grip of a devastating intermittent civil war for over thirty years after 1562. From the dominant, aggressive power in European international politics, France almost overnight became a victim state and the cockpit of contending forces: Calvinism versus Catholicism, feudal and provincial rights versus monarchical centralization, English intervention versus Spanish intervention.

The eleven years between the death of Henry VIII (1547) and the accession of Queen Elizabeth (1558) are sometimes called a "barren interlude" in English history, and so they were perhaps from the point of view of political development. But Elizabeth's caution and achievements cannot be understood apart from the violent swings of the religious pendulum under her younger brother, Edward VI (1547–1553), and her older sister, Mary (1553–1558), during this interlude. Under the boy-king Edward, the Protestant party gained control of the government and swung England more clearly into the Protestant camp. It was a strange and confused six years in which Archbishop Thomas Cranmer gave his countrymen the English Prayer Book, that masterpiece of English style and sane religious compromise, while some of the most unscrupulous adventurers in English history were scheming to exclude Mary the Catholic, daughter of Catherine of Aragon, from the throne in favor of their puppet, Lady Jane Grey. The Protestant reformers were a small minority, and their cause was not helped by their association with political adventurers who were bringing back the rule of feudal cliques to

English government. The mass of the English people were happy when Mary made good her claim to the throne in 1553.

Their happiness was short lived, however. Everyone knew that Mary, the daughter of Catherine of Aragon, would undo the work of her father and brother and restore England's obedience to the pope. There was no real opposition to the reconciliation as such. Significantly, the Act of Parliament which restored the papal supremacy in England (1554–1555) also guaranteed to hundreds of laymen the possession of monastic lands confiscated, and distributed, by Henry VIII—just as the Peace of Augsburg the same year guaranteed property rights in confiscated church property in Protestant lands in Germany. But Mary made two grave mistakes at least from the political point of view (it should be said that she was a conscientious woman, and no politician). She eagerly married Philip of Spain in spite of the patriotic protests of her Council, her Parliament, and her people; and she allowed her restored Catholic bishops to burn about three hundred persons for Protestant heresy, most of them (except for Cranmer and his associates) obscure, ordinary people. Whether deservedly or not, Spain and Catholic fanaticism became indissolubly associated in the English mind, and the Protestantism which Cranmer could not sell to the majority of Englishmen when he was in power began to become the mark of an English patriot in the fiery persecution of Mary's reign.

When Elizabeth came to the throne in 1558, it seemed likely that papal supremacy was through for good in England. The young queen had to move carefully because of fear of the power of Spain, but as the daughter of Anne Boleyn she had no choice but to steer England cautiously back into the Protestant fold. The Elizabethan religious settlement was a compromise—more stable and longer lived than anyone would have guessed in the early years of the reign. The papal supremacy was once more rejected, but it was left very vague just where ecclesiastical authority was lodged in England. In succeeding years the queen, Parliament, and Convocation all claimed something of the pope's powers, but in practice the queen always had the last word. Cranmer's Prayer Book was again made the basis of the liturgy, and 39 Articles of Faith were drawn up, both documents drawing upon many streams of Christian tradition, from Catholicism and Lutheranism to Zwinglianism and Calvinism. Thanks to the way the breach with Rome originally took place (and perhaps thanks also to national temperament), the English were never so concerned about religious belief as they were about practice. Whether there should be bishops in the church, what they should wear, and whether there should be an "altar" or a "communion table"—these were the questions which agitated Englishmen, not salvation by faith and predestination. The Anglican ideal, never quite put into words, was to build a broad national church, closely linked to the secular state, which would exclude nobody but fanatical Romanists and religious radicals, and would rely not only upon the Bible but also upon tradition and reason for religious authority. The comprehensive Protestantism of Queen Elizabeth's religious settlement at least laid the basis for realization of this ideal.

The Hegemony of Spain

In the later sixteenth century military, political, and to some extent cultural predominance passed to Spain under

Philip II (1556–1598). Spanish military organization—with its balanced regiments of pikes, short swords, and harquebuses—Spanish battle tactics, and Spanish morale were the best in Europe. Spanish soldiers were the hardiest on the continent (they came from a climate which has been described as "nine months' winter and three months' hell"). Among the Spanish nobility, which included a large number of *hidalgos* or gentry, it was not fashionable to work, but it was fashionable to fight. So there was always a supply of men and officers for the army and of adventurers to help build a New Castile across the Atlantic. The monarchical bureaucracy which Philip developed at Madrid became the model, for better or worse, of the administrative practices of the next century. It was slow, cumbersome, and complicated. "If death came from Spain," wrote the king's viceroy in Naples, "we should live to a very great age." But it was modern for its day and motivated by Philip's passion for thoroughness, orderliness, and justice. He never forgot his father's advice to him: "Depend on no one but yourself." The result was an overcentralized bureaucracy which nevertheless bound Castile, Aragon, Portugal (under the Spanish crown from 1580 to 1640), most of Italy, the Netherlands, and Spanish America into a formidable empire until the long decline of Spanish power set in toward the end of the century. Spanish cultural ascendancy followed the peak of military and political power: the author of *Don Quixote*, Cervantes, and the painter, El Greco, died some fifteen years after the close of the century. That curious combination of the sacred and secular in literary and artistic style which we call the Baroque had many roots, but the strongest were in Spain. With the decline of France after 1559, in other words, Spain became the first example in European history of the temporary "hegemony," or predominance in power and leadership, of one of several sovereign states in a system usually characterized by a balance of power.

The reasons for this hegemony were partly material, partly spiritual. Spain's command of the gold and silver of the New World was undoubtedly the main sinew of her strength. The flow of precious metals enabled the Spanish government simultaneously to maintain troops on the Danube and the Rhine, ships in the Mediterranean and the Caribbean (although the government went bankrupt twice in Philip's reign). The inflation which the influx of bullion brought about was at first stimulating to the industry and agriculture of the country, and the early sixteenth century was a period of prosperity in Spain. Some scholars maintain that the Spanish economy remained vigorous and healthy till almost the end of the century, but others see a decline setting in by 1580 or even earlier. Spain seemed destined to share the fate of King Midas, who died of starvation when his wish that all he touched should turn to gold was fulfilled. The nation in effect used its treasure to pay its armies abroad and to import the manufactured goods which its own industries could not turn out so cheaply (because inflation in Spain always outran the price rise elsewhere). This hurt native industry, and in the end foreign imports and heavy taxation all but ruined Spanish production. Spain was left with nothing much but its gold and silver, and even this supply began to peter out in the next century.

There are also nonmaterial reasons for the brief but brilliant predominance of Spain under Philip II. The rulers and the ruling classes in sixteenth-century Spain had a sense of destiny. They believed that it had fallen to the Spanish people to assume the burden of reviving and realizing the Christian empire of the Middle Ages. The Spaniards at first did not like it when their young king Charles was elected Holy Roman Emperor in 1519. The following year the king-emperor had a spokesman explain to the Castilian Cortes (or representative assembly) what this meant to Spain:

Now the ancient glory of Spain has returned, as in the days when the old writers said of her that while other nations sent tributes to Rome it was her happy lot to send emperors. She sent Trajan, Hadrian, and Theodosius, and now the Empire has come to seek an Emperor in Spain, and by God's grace our Spanish King is made King of the Romans and Emperor of the world.[1]

Charles explained further that Spain would be the "fortress, strength, treasure, and sword" of his European policy, and that his true motive was to defeat the enemies of the Holy Catholic Faith. On the whole he lived up to this program: he spent his life opposing the Turk and the Protestant, and after his abdication he returned to die in Spain as a symbol of his attachment to the center of his empire. It was a bitter disappointment to Philip that the imperial title went not to him but to his uncle Ferdinand, and it was twice rumored in his reign that he was about to take the title of Emperor of the Indies. But he and his nobility developed a compensatory Spanish imperialism which grew directly out of his father's theory. In essence it was Spanish nationalism combined with a sense of messianic mission. Spain was the nation divinely chosen to save Christendom from the Turkish infidel and from the Protestant heretic, to carry the Gospel

[1] Quoted by permission of The Macmillan Company from R. B. Merriman, *Rise of the Spanish Empire* (New York, 1925), III, 49–50.

to the New World and to restore the true Catholic faith in the Old. It is difficult to measure the part this messianic faith played in the exploits of Spanish conquistadores in America and Spanish armies in Europe, but it was undoubtedly considerable.

It must be added immediately that this was a *Spanish*, not a *papal* imperialism. Philip began his reign by fighting a war with the pope in Italy; he opposed papal policy at the Council of Trent; and he never allowed the pope to have any say in ecclesiastical appointments or jurisdiction in Spain. In fact, he was almost as antipapal as Henry VIII himself. But he was genuinely religious and devoted to Catholicism as all his countrymen were. Generally Philip was in close alliance with the pope on Turkish or Protestant problems. Spain was the center of both Catholic Reformation and Counter Reformation, but Philip himself was never in full sympathy with the Jesuits or the Fathers of Trent. In practice his policy was always to choose whatever course would benefit Spain, but he easily persuaded himself that this course was automatically the best for Catholic Christendom. The grim, grey Escorial which he erected for his residence near Madrid—half palace, half monastery—was a symbol of this strange blending of secular and religious motives in himself and in his imperial ideal.

The first half of his reign was mainly occupied with measures to counter the Turk. Here Philip was simply taking up the centuries-long Spanish crusade against the Moslems. By 1560 the Christians had been driven from nearly all their footholds on the North African coast. When the Moriscoes or "converted" Moors in southeastern Spain rose in revolt in 1567, the fear ran through the country that the Moslems of North Africa would use the rebellion as an entering wedge for an Islamic reconquest of the peninsula. The revolt was quelled, however, and in 1571 Philip's navy, aided by Venetian, Genoese, and papal ships, won a decisive victory over a Turkish fleet at Lepanto in the Gulf of Corinth. This victory marked the end of Turkish naval predominance in the Mediterranean and freed the Spanish to turn elsewhere. Meanwhile Spanish troops had been active all through the century in helping various other armies to hold the line against the Turks in the Danube valley. Until 1572 Philip and Spain were following their imperial destiny mainly in checking the expansion of the other great empire, the Ottoman, at the opposite end of the Mediterranean.

It was not till the second half of his reign that Philip realized that the real danger lay in northwestern Europe. The Protestants were apparently growing stronger in France, though they were obviously a minority. Philip could not allow France to go Protestant, and there might be great gain for Spain from fishing in the troubled waters north of the Pyrenees. The Netherlands were in open revolt against Spanish rule, and the brutal attempts of Philip's ablest henchman, the duke of Alva, to crush the opposition (1567–1573) had not succeeded. If the Netherlands were lost, the blow to Spanish economy and morale would be very severe. Finally, England was looming ever larger on the Spanish horizon as English freebooters made more and more daring inroads on Spanish commerce in the New World. Philip had offered Elizabeth his hand shortly after her accession, hoping to keep England in the Hapsburg orbit, but after the pope had formally excommunicated the queen in 1570, the king of Spain saw it might be better to try to unseat her from her throne. The Anglo-Spanish alliance, which went back to 1489 and was firmly based on English economic interests in the Netherlands, had been first shaken by the unpopular marriage of Philip and Mary. By the 1570's it was seriously threatened by Anglo-Spanish rivalry in America and in the rebellious Netherlands. There was much to gain and still more to lose for Spain in the North, and it was here that Philip turned his attention after Lepanto.

In Philip II's struggle with the Protestant forces of northern Europe there was no glorious Lepanto at the end of the road. Instead there was the bitter defeat of the "Invincible Armada," the Spanish fleet sent northward in 1588 to hold the English Channel so that Spanish troops under the duke of Parma could be ferried across from the Netherlands for the conquest of England. The defeat of the Armada by English seamanship and "Protestant weather" decided the fate of Philip's efforts to crush out Protestantism in England and the Netherlands and to assure the victory of the extreme Catholic party in France. The high-built Spanish galleons crowded with Spain's finest foot soldiers and helplessly riddled by shot from Drake's faster-moving English vessels were somehow symbolic of the hollow brilliance of Spanish imperialism.

The Spanish people look back on the conscientious and imperturbable "Philip the Prudent" as their greatest king because better than any other he embodied the dream of Spain's messianic mission to restore Catholic Christendom in its moment of greatest peril. But when he died in 1598 his country was exhausted, its economy on the decline, half the Netherlands lost, France restored to unity and strength, and England ready to contest the Spanish monopoly in America. His reign was a glorious failure.

The Trial of France

From 1562 to 1593 France underwent her severest trial between the Hundred Years' War and her great Revolution of 1789. For thirty years the whole land was torn by intermittent civil wars of terrible ferocity, now concentrating in pitched battles which decided nothing, now degenerating into street fights, local massacres, and individual atrocities, now breaking out into destruction of images in churches or simply into wanton destruction of homes and crops. Uneasy truces brought temporary lulls, but there was no restoration of public order until a generation of bloodshed had so sickened the common people and ruling classes alike that all sides were willing to accept a peace of compromise.

These wars are called the French "Wars of Religion," but this title does not quite describe their complexity. Religion was certainly the main cause. Although almost everywhere a minority doctrine, Calvinism had taken root in almost every important town in France by 1560 and was strong in Paris and in the cities around the periphery of the country such as Rouen in the north, La Rochelle in the west, and the towns of the Rhone Valley in the south. Furthermore, members of the lesser nobility had become converted and had carried with them whole districts, including the peasantry, where their influence was strong. Finally the Huguenots (as the French Calvinists were called) had made important converts among the highest nobility, particularly the family of Bourbon, kings of Navarre and closely related to the French royal family itself, and the family of Chastillon, of whom Admiral Coligny was the ablest representative. The Huguenots boasted some 2,500 organized churches in 1561, all of course strictly illegal. They probably never numbered more than 1,200,000 in a population of about 16,000,000 (some estimates are much higher), but they were a determined and dedicated minority, sure that God was on their side, and confident of sympathy and perhaps help from abroad—from Geneva, Germany, the Netherlands, and England.

The mass of the people were still Catholic, and most important of all, the monarchy was firmly Catholic, as were the theologians of the University of Paris and the lawyers of the Paris Parlement. In the Concordat of Bologna of 1516 the French monarchs had gained all the control they needed over the church in France. They were often as independent as Philip II in their attitude toward the pope, but none of them happened to find personal and dynastic reasons for breaking with papal jurisdiction as Henry VIII did. The steady adherence to Catholicism of the monarchy and the government until the very end of the civil wars is the most important reason why France today is predominantly Catholic rather than Protestant. French Calvinism failed to capture the government until the religious lines were hardened and until it was too late for such an event to be decisive.

The leaders of the extreme Catholic party in the 1550's were the family of Guise. In 1559 Mary Stuart, niece of the duke of Guise and soon to be queen of Scots, was married briefly to the young French king, Francis II, who died in 1560. This gave the Guises the kind of direct personal power at the court of Catherine de' Medici which sent a thrill of terror through the whole Huguenot community. And when some troops of the duke of Guise happened on a Huguenot congregation at Vassy and massacred three hundred of them in March 1562, it was the signal for confused religious and civil strife to break out all over France.

From the very beginning the religious issue acted as detonator for other explosive issues which had nothing necessarily to do with the mutual fear and hatred of Catholics and Protestants. Towns and provinces, particularly in the south, which had long unsuccessfully resisted the inexorable trend toward monarchical centralization now broke out into rebellion against a weakened monarchy. Feudal nobles who had been occupied in the dynastic wars of Hapsburg and Valois until the peace of 1559 now turned their turbulent energies into domestic feuds, such as that between the Guises and the Chastillons. Finally foreign powers intervened in France, either to help coreligionists or to slice off a bit of territory from a crippled French government. In the early years of the wars Philip II threatened to intervene on the side of the Guises, and Elizabeth of England did intervene on the side of the Huguenots. Although both became more cautious for a time, the Wars of Religion ended with English and Spanish armies on French soil. The French Wars of Religion were social, dynastic, and international, as well as religious in origin and character.

France in her time of trouble illustrated more poignantly perhaps than any other nation the characteristic sixteenth-century form of the ancient rivalry between church and state for men's allegiance. The claim of religious belief on a zealous Calvinist or Catholic dwarfed or excluded the claim of the dynastic state on his loyalties. Huguenots, for instance, often had more in common with Dutch Calvinists and English Presbyterians than they had with fellow Frenchmen who were Catholics. In 1565 a close friend of the Guises remarked to the Spanish ambassador:

Nowadays Catholic princes must not proceed as they once did. At one time friends and enemies were distinguished by the frontiers of provinces and kingdoms, and were called Italians, Germans, French, Spaniards, English, and the like; now we must say Catholics and heretics, and a Catholic prince must consider all Catholics of all countries as his friends, just as the heretics consider all heretics as friends and subjects, whether they are their own vassals or not.[2]

Like twentieth-century ideologies, religion in the sixteenth century demanded loyalty to a cause higher than either the dynasty or the nation. At one time or another during the wars in France, both Calvinist and Catholic political pamphleteers argued for constitutional resistance to monarchical tyranny, for provincial "states' rights," and even for republicanism and tyrannicide. Religious truth was more important to them than strong civil government, and they were not afraid to be called traitors or rebels.

From the very beginning the regent, Catherine de' Medici, was the center of a small party which believed the exact opposite of all this. They put politics before religion and thought that no truth was worth the cost of civil war. These *politiques*, as they were called, were to win out in the end, but only after both sides had become exhausted by bloodletting. As early as 1563 government edicts foreshadowed something of the ultimate solution: freedom of conscience, freedom of worship for the Calvinist minority, and guarantees that neither side would break the peace. During the 1560's the Huguenots successfully held their own, even if they lost most of the pitched battles they fought. In the summer of 1572, however, the Guises persuaded Catherine and

[2] Erich Marcks, *Die Zusammenkunft von Bayonne* (Strasbourg, 1889), p. 14.

the young king, Charles IX (1560–1574), that the Huguenot problem could be solved at one blow by the murder of the Calvinist leaders. On the eve of St. Bartholomew's Day (August 24), Coligny and others were done to death in Paris, and the fury spread throughout France during the next ten days. When it was over, more than ten thousand Huguenots had been massacred. This was the most spectacular of the innumerable atrocities on both sides which made any permanent settlement impossible until after almost thirty years of strife.

By the 1580's several elements in the picture had changed. The Huguenot strength was less scattered geographically, concentrated chiefly in the south and the west. It was no longer growing. The extreme Catholic party had formed the Holy League in 1576 which by now was as dangerous to the integrity of the monarchy as the Huguenots had ever been, supported as it was by Philip of Spain. Religious tempers still ran high, but there was an increasing number who subscribed to the argument of the *politiques* or who listened to the cool wisdom of the quizzical Montaigne, whose *Essays* began to appear in 1580. "A thousand times," Montaigne wrote, he had gone to bed expecting to be "betrayed or murdered before morning, and bargaining with fortune that it be done without terror or lingering." Such a state of affairs was utterly senseless, he argued. "There is no enmity like the Christian." But "after all," he said, "it is setting a very high price on one's conjectures to burn a man alive for them." He was speaking of witchcraft, but to every sort of fanaticism he offered the antidote of a sane and humane skepticism. By now there were many who were ready to follow him.

The Wars of Religion ended like a Shakespearean tragedy.

In 1588 Henry Duke of Guise was murdered by order of King Henry III (1574–1589), the last of Catherine de' Medici's sickly sons. In 1589 King Henry himself was murdered by a Dominican friar, and the gallant Henry of Navarre, a Bourbon and a Protestant, became king. It took him five years to make good his title, be crowned at Chartres, and re-enter his capital city, Paris—and he had to renounce his Protestantism and become a Catholic (1593) in order to do it. The majority of his people were still Catholic, as were the Parlement, the university, and the League, which controlled Paris. Henry IV was a *politique* in the best sense, convinced that the peace of the nation was worth a Mass. His conversion at first outraged everyone, but in the end it opened the way to the recovery of France, which was far along the road to renewed economic and political strength by the time of his death in 1610.

In 1598, over the protests of the Catholic clergy, the Parlement, and many of the cities of France, Henry IV published the Edict of Nantes. This granted liberty of conscience to the Huguenots without restriction and liberty of worship in two places in each local district except large towns, where services had to be held outside the walls (in the case of Paris, twelve miles outside). Protestants were given all the civil and legal rights held by Catholics. As guarantee, mixed courts representing both Protestants and Catholics were set up, and two hundred fortified towns were left in the hands of Huguenot governors and garrisons. The Edict was thus a compromise; like the Peace of Augsburg, it recognized a religious stalemate. Further, it allowed a kind of "state within a state" to exist. It broke with the ancient principle of *"un roi, une loi, une foi"* by restoring the monarchy and the law but leaving France divided be-

tween a Catholic majority and a Calvinist minority. This
implied that the peaceful coexistence of two faiths in one
state was perfectly possible. The grant of freedom of conscience and worship was declared "perpetual and irrevocable." But the Edict was a free grant by a restored monarchy.
Less than a century later Louis XIV, a stronger if not a wiser
king, would retract the measure of toleration which the
first Bourbon monarch had granted.

Out of the French civil wars came a welter of political
writings, but it is perhaps no wonder that the tracts which
had most influence on the next century were those that
preached the importance of authority and strong government, not the treatises by Calvinists and Jesuits, which ad-
vocated resistance to tyranny whenever its own party was
out of power. Jean Bodin (1530–1596), the most powerful
political thinker of the century and author of *The Republic*
(1576), lived through the Wars of Religion. He came out
with the conviction that sovereignty—the power "to lay
down the law to all subjects without their consent"—must
rightfully reside somewhere in every well-ordered state,
preferably in the monarch. Bodin was a lawyer and a patriot
who was trying to find a rational justification for strong
government in the midst of civil war without throwing over
entirely the best of mediaeval thinking about legal restraints
on arbitrary power. But lesser thinkers were soon dropping
his qualifications and speaking about the divine right of
kings—a right bestowed on hereditary monarchs not by the
pope of Rome, or by any company of self-appointed saints
like the Calvinists, or (for that matter) by the people at
large, but by God himself. The king, then, was responsible
to no one but God. The theory of the divine right of kings
was the answer to the threat of anarchy growing out of

the claims of absolutist religious organizations such as the Catholic and the Calvinist to make and unmake secular governments. To the Catholic claim that only the vicar of Christ has true divine right, and to the Calvinist claim that no human being can claim absolute power because only God is sovereign, men of the early seventeenth century who lived through a generation of religious and civil strife began to answer, the king is God's representative on earth —obey him and him alone.

The Revolt of the Netherlands

While France was undergoing her Wars of Religion, the Netherlands were plunged into a revolt against Spanish rule which proved to be even more furious and destructive than the troubles in France. Religion, patriotism, and economic grievances all played their part in the origins of the revolt, together with Spanish mistakes in policy. In the struggle the new forces of Calvinism and national sentiment were strangely allied with the older forces of feudal privilege and provincial rights against the steady pressure of Spanish attempts to crush out heresy and to centralize and unify the provinces.

The Netherlands consisted of seventeen provinces which had been gathered together over two centuries by the dukes of Burgundy and their heirs, the Hapsburgs Maximilian and Charles V. The Walloon provinces, which constituted the southern third of this territory, were French-speaking, the remainder Dutch-speaking. The northern third was geographically isolated by the line of the rivers Rhine and Meuse as they bend westward to empty into the North Sea. In the middle third was the largest and most important province, Brabant, with the Netherlands' capital city (Brussels), the commercial center (Antwerp), and the chief university town (Louvain). To the west of Brabant was the province of Flanders, to the northwest Zealand, to the north Holland. These four provinces clustering about the mouths of the great rivers were the heart of the Netherlands, the second great center (after Northern Italy) of urban civilization in sixteenth-century Europe.

It was the tragedy of the Netherlands that their rulers were foreigners. Emperor Charles V had been born there, it is true, but he often sacrificed the Netherlands to his larger European interests and became more and more Spanish as he grew older. His son Philip did not even speak the languages of his Netherlandish subjects, never lived in the provinces after 1559, and in his monastic palace in Spain never attempted to imagine the true feelings of his restless subjects almost a thousand miles away. The Hapsburgs had centralized the administration of the seventeen provinces, developed the States-General or assembly which represented all of them, and unintentionally given the higher nobility and upper middle classes a sense of Netherlandish patriotism. But since the rulers themselves were "foreigners," the rising national sentiment in the provinces had no such dynastic focus as it had in England and France in their native kings. The result was a growing tension between rulers and subjects which was increased by economic and religious grievances. The merchants and manufacturers of the Netherlands were fabulously prosperous, but they resented the constant demands made upon them to support Hapsburg wars in which they often had little interest. As for religion, the most characteristic native contribution of the Netherlands was the tolerant, liberal, Christian Humanism represented by Erasmus of Rotterdam and some other Netherlanders. But

Lutheranism took early root in the provinces, as did Anabaptism. Both of these were overshadowed by the rapid
spread of Calvinism in the 1550's and 1560's. From the beginning most severe repressive measures were used against
heresy by the government, with two results: the people of
the Netherlands developed an ineradicable hatred of religious persecution, and heresy continued to grow.

Shortly after he left for Spain in 1559, Philip II developed
a statesmanlike plan for reorganizing the Catholic Church
in the Netherlands by excluding French influence and setting up new bishoprics under bishops appointed by the local
government (as they were in Spain). The fact that such a
sensible plan as this to reorganize the church along more
modern lines aroused a universal howl of protest should
have warned the king how ticklish the situation was. In
the new plan the clergy and nobility saw infringement of
their rights and privileges, and the middle classes feared a
better-organized inquisition. In the summer of 1566 a wave
of iconoclasm or image-breaking spread like wildfire all
over the provinces. The Protestant, particularly the Calvinist, saw only idolatry in the veneration of saints and relics,
only superstition in the belief that the Mass was somehow
a renewed sacrifice of Christ on the altar worked by the
priest. So when Calvinists rioted anywhere, and particularly
in the Netherlands, the images of the saints in stone
and stained glass, not to speak of altars and even priests
themselves, were the first objects of their fury. The riots
of 1566 were the work of a small minority, but they were
the first open step toward forty years of revolutionary
activity.

Philip's answer was the severest and most brutal kind of
repression. For six years (1567–1573) his agent the duke

of Alva made a shambles of the country, confiscating, burning, and executing. He did what the Calvinist minority was unable to do—he united almost all classes in all seventeen provinces in hatred of Spain. This was the result particularly of his imposing a 10-per-cent sales tax (modeled on Spanish practice) which well-nigh ruined the trade of the country. Most of the people were still firmly Catholic and still loyal to Philip as the anointed ruler of the land (if not to Alva). But with economic depression, religious persecution, and national humiliation staring them in the face and with no apparent prospect of relief, they were soon driven to organized rebellion.

The revolution began in the north, in Holland and Zealand, which carried on the burden of rebellion alone for four years (1572–1576). These were the provinces in most intimate contact with the sea, and it was the Sea Beggars (or anti-Spanish pirates and privateers) who were the strength of their resistance. The northern provinces found a leader in William of Orange, one of the greatest nobles and largest landowners in the Netherlands. In the welter of scheming or overbearing wielders of power in sixteenth-century politics, William stands out almost in a class by himself—far-seeing, fair-minded, gifted with almost incredible patience, imperturbably tolerant in religion, and as selfless as a practical statesman can ever be. Brought up a Catholic, married to a Lutheran, William was almost inevitably drawn into the Calvinist camp as the struggle developed, but he was first a patriot and a humanitarian, never a sectarian. He called upon his countrymen "to restore the whole fatherland to its old liberty and prosperity out of the clutches of the Spanish vultures and wolves." Although he failed in the end to hold the whole nation together, he guided the course of the revolution from 1572 until an assassin's bullet cut short his life in 1584.

As early as 1573 a small Calvinist minority established complete political control over Holland and Zealand, for the simple reason that they were best organized and mentally equipped to carry on the war against Spanish tyranny. The fanaticism and intolerance of this minority was often a trial to William, but in 1576 it seemed as if he had attained his highest goal when the whole States-General approved what was called the Pacification of Ghent, under the shock of a terrible sack of Antwerp by Spanish troops in which seven thousand patriots lost their lives. The Pacification was an agreement between Holland and Zealand, on the one hand, and the provinces of the States-General, on the other, to stand together until the Spanish soldiers were expelled and to respect religious differences. In this last respect it was like the Peace of Augsburg, an agreement to live and let live with respect to religion. Apparently Orange's dream of a United Netherlands, free of Spain and tolerant in religion, was about to come true.

Tragedy stalked the Pacification of Ghent, however. The Calvinists, though always a minority, were just as strong in the cities of Brabant and Flanders as they were in Holland. The example of Calvinist political dictatorship in Holland made Calvinists elsewhere restive and envious. A Calvinist coup d'état took place in Ghent in 1578, and the Catholics everywhere took fright. Early in 1579 the Walloon provinces formed a Catholic Union at Arras, and almost at the same time a Protestant Union of the provinces north of the great rivers (with some cities south of the line) was signed at Utrecht. The Union of Utrecht of 1579 was the direct origin of the independent United Provinces or Dutch

Netherlands, which formally renounced their allegiance to Philip II in 1581. Religion was the rock, therefore, on which the unity of the Netherlands foundered. There was no geographical localization of Calvinism when the revolt started, except that it was predominantly an urban affair. But as the fighting progressed—a peculiarly atrocious sort of fighting, with whole towns sometimes put to the torch and sword—the fact that the Spanish oppressors were Catholic and their toughest opponents Calvinist had its effect. Patriots had to become Calvinist, in sympathy at least, or submit to Spanish rule to preserve their Catholicism, as the Walloons did. Above all, the issue was finally determined by force— by the accidents of foreign intervention, Spanish and Dutch military genius, and geography.

After Alva's departure in 1573 the prostrate Netherlands became the prize of a three-cornered duel between Spain, France, and England. Both France and England were afraid of Spain, but they were also afraid of each other. The result was that their intervention was usually halting and ineffective. Catherine de' Medici's youngest son, the duke of Anjou as he was later called, was the agent of French intervention until his death in 1584, but he played a confusing game of deceit and never drew any effective support from his own divided country. In 1585 Elizabeth sent the earl of Leicester to the Netherlands with an English army which was of some but not much benefit to the rebels. Both Anjou and Leicester at one time or another schemed to step into Philip's shoes as ruler of the Netherlands, and both lost as many battles as they won. The dominating figure in the Netherlands after his appointment as Philip's representative in 1578 was Alexander Farnese, duke of Parma. Parma was a first-rate general and a smart diplomatist. It was mainly his genius which was responsible for the reduction once more of all the provinces south of the great rivers to Spanish rule. Beyond the rivers he could not operate effectively: geography was the chief defense of the United Provinces in the north. Furthermore, the defeat of the Armada (1588) and the accession of Henry IV in France (1589) were decisive for the ultimate freedom of the Dutch Netherlands. After the Armada they were always open to English support, and after the accession of Henry, Philip kept Parma busy invading northeastern France in a vain attempt to prevent the Protestant Henry IV from consolidating his power. Parma died in 1592, a much frustrated man, and the rebels under William's talented son, Maurice of Nassau, began to push a defensible frontier somewhat south of the rivers. It was on this line that a truce was finally concluded between the United Provinces and Spain in 1609, bringing to a close over a generation of bloodshed; and it is there that the frontier between Holland and Belgium lies today.

The revolt of the Netherlands has long interested Americans, who have seen in it close parallels to their own revolution. William of Orange plays the part of Washington, Philip II of George III. There are the same general grievances—economic, political, and sentimental—the same problem of uniting seventeen or thirteen separate political units in a common struggle. The parallel breaks down in two important respects, however. Thanks to the religious issue, the revolt of the Netherlands was a far more brutal and venomous struggle than the American. And in the case of the Netherlands, only half the country won its independence from foreign rule. It was as if the American Revolution had ended with all the colonies northeast of the Hudson still in English hands. The Dutch Netherlands went on to experience their most glorious age of commercial prosperity, naval glory, and cultural achievement in the seventeenth century. Meanwhile the Spanish Netherlands sank back into apathy. There was no necessary reason for the differing fates of the two halves, as the Dutch historian Geyl insists, beyond the ability of Parma and the configuration of the rivers.

Elizabethan England

While the other major states of Europe were exhausting their energies in civil or foreign wars, England was husbanding her strength in twenty-six important years of peace (1559–1585). The nation owed these years of calm to its ruler, Queen Elizabeth (1558–1603).

The Protestant exiles who streamed back to England from Geneva and Strasbourg and Frankfort after the death of Mary the Catholic were not peaceful men. They wished to purify the Anglican Church of all practices which still savored of Rome and so later became known as Puritans. They disliked everything from priestly vestments and kneeling at communion to the use of altars and the institution of episcopacy. They were a minority, but a vigorous and important one. They dominated Parliament whenever it was called (the queen summoned ten parliaments in thirteen sessions during her forty-four years on the throne), were strong among the lower clergy, and had powerful friends in the government like the earl of Leicester and Sir Francis Walsingham. Their politically minded members constantly pressed for an aggressive and pro-Protestant foreign policy in support of the Presbyterians in Scotland, the Huguenots in France, and the Calvinists in the Netherlands.

On the other side of the religious fence, the Catholics

were a generally demoralized and dispirited group after the death of Mary. Somewhere between the accession of Elizabeth and the arrival of the first Jesuit missionaries in 1579, the Catholics sank for the first time to a minority in England, thanks to neglect by the papacy, the tolerant policy of the English government, and the growth of national sentiment. But after the papal bull of 1570, which excommunicated the queen and deposed her from her throne, good Catholics had in theory to choose between their religion and their loyalty to their queen. From the 1570's onward, as the Counter Reformation gained headway all over Europe, the Catholics in England became a small but reinvigorated and potentially dangerous minority, hoping against hope for the restoration of the papal obedience, perhaps by French or Spanish arms.

England, in other words, had all the combustible materials which in the case of France and the Netherlands were to lead to civil war and involvement in international conflict. But Elizabeth and her chief minister, Sir William Cecil, were what the French called *politiques*. Elizabeth was first a patriot and second (or third) a Protestant Christian. She said she had no intention of opening windows into men's minds, and all her life she consistently concerned herself with men's acts, not their opinions. This meant that so long as Catholics did not commit treason and so long as Puritans did not infringe on her royal prerogatives, they might think as they pleased. In her foreign policy the interests of England, not of international Protestantism, always came first. Her first and deepest impulse in a crisis was to do nothing, to let time solve the problem for her. She often drove her ministers to distraction by her apparent inability to make up her mind. Her instinct was never to close doors, always to preserve possibilities, always to encourage people on all sides of a controversy to believe that she would eventually do what they hoped she would do. "Among all great rulers," wrote the English historian J. R. Seeley, "it is the distinction of Elizabeth to have shown how much may be achieved by simply allowing full play to the influence of time." [3]

It is hard to point to any positive, constructive policies which were Elizabeth's, but there are a great many things she might have done, and did not do, which would have made the Elizabethan Age impossible. She kept the ebullient energies of her people in check until the time was ripe for them to burst forth and then released them, not because she wanted to but because she could not help it. At home she skillfully encouraged industry and trade, recognized care of the poor as a national responsibility, kept the Puritans from liquidating the Catholics and upsetting the orderly regime of bishops, and managed to make herself fabulously popular, even with her Puritan political opponents. Abroad she steered England cautiously through the stormy waters of the early years of her reign until the nation was ready for the glorious triumphs of her later years.

The chief threat to England in 1558, as it had been for over two hundred years, was France. Mary of Guise was regent of Scotland, her daughter Mary Stuart was married to the French dauphin, and the Guise family thus seemed to have England caught in a Franco-Scottish vise, an ancient device of the French. Within a few short years the whole picture had changed. John Knox, trained in Geneva, together with his followers among the Scottish nobility, had worked a Calvinist revolution in Scotland with the support of Elizabeth, and France was on the eve of her civil wars.

[3] *The Growth of British Policy* (Cambridge, 1897), I, 247.

After the death of her mother and her husband, Mary Stuart, now queen of Scots, returned to Scotland (1561). But within six years her utter lack of sympathy with both the religion and the national sensibilities of her people together with her marital mistakes cost her the throne, and she found herself an exile in England, much to Elizabeth's embarrassment. The old Scottish-French alliance was permanently broken, and the way was cleared for Mary's infant son James to become king of both Scotland and England after the death of his mother and of Elizabeth. France was never a serious threat to England from 1560 to the end of the century, and there were brief periods when the two ancient enemies were formal allies of each other.

For over half a century Spain had been England's ally. The bond was strengthened when Charles V became both lord of the Netherlands and king of Spain. In spite of the strains in the alliance caused by Henry VIII's falling-out with Catherine of Aragon and by the unpopularity of Philip of Spain as Mary's husband, Spain was still Elizabeth's one powerful ally when she became queen. Friction began to develop rapidly, however, in the 1570's, and during the 1580's the breaking point was reached. It now seems inevitable that England and Spain should eventually have become rivals. When the Atlantic replaced the Mediterranean as the chief highway of European ocean-borne commerce, the Iberian peninsula and the British Isles acquired a new importance. With France crippled by domestic troubles, Spain's first dangerous rival for the trade and treasure of the New World was England. English privateers were selling slaves in Spanish America in the 1560's, and by the 1570's Sir Francis Drake and his fellow Sea Dogs were becoming the terror of the Spanish Main, as the Dutch

Sea Beggars were of the waters around continental Europe. Spain and England were at war on the high seas long before there was any breach of the peace in Europe.

To trade rivalry were added two other major causes of Anglo-Spanish friction. The first, as already suggested, was the revolt of the Netherlands. From the beginning the sympathies of most Englishmen were with the rebels, and as the northern provinces began to establish their independence, the economic ties between English and Dutch merchants reinforced the sentimental bond. The final cause of friction was Spanish interference in English domestic affairs. If the English were the aggressors on the seas, the Spanish were the aggressors in the matter of fostering plots and subversive groups in the rival state. Between 1568 and 1572 Elizabeth was faced with a series of risings and plots which shook her throne. The manpower came from the Catholic nobility of the north of England, and the focus of every plot was Mary Queen of Scots, Elizabeth's heir apparent and semiprisoner in England. Behind the conspiracies was the Spanish ambassador in London. These plots, together with the revolt of Holland and Zealand and the Massacre of St. Bartholomew's in 1572, combined to push Elizabeth into a foreign policy she disliked, namely the underhand support of Protestant rebellion in France and the Netherlands in order to cripple the Catholic Spanish power which was threatening her at home. In 1584–1585 things came to a head. The assassination of William of Orange and the death of the duke of Anjou (lately Elizabeth's instrument in her foreign policy) forced the queen to intervene openly and actively in the Netherlands to prevent the rebels' failure, and in France to insure the accession and success of Henry of Navarre. At almost the same time Mary Queen of Scots became involved in her last Spanish plot, and in 1587 Elizabeth was finally persuaded to send her to the block.

In 1585 undeclared war broke out between England and Spain. By the 1590's England was involved in ventures so large and numerous that they would have broken her strength a half-century before: a maritime war to the death with Spain which culminated but did not end with the defeat of the Armada in 1588, and three land wars, in northern France, in the Netherlands, and in Ireland, where the Jesuits had revived Irish morale and the Spanish were actively supporting a widespread rebellion against English rule. (English suppression of the Irish rebellion was as brutal as, but more effective than, Alva's bloody work in the Netherlands.) The war at sea broke Spanish naval supremacy for good, but proved that it was no more possible for England to conquer Spain from the sea than for Spain to conquer England. The legend of Spanish greatness survived to terrify Protestant courts in the seventeenth century, but that greatness had vanished in fact before England and Spain made peace shortly after Elizabeth's death.

Before her death the drain upon English financial and human resources became evident in the increasing unruliness of Parliament and the difficulty of raising men and money. But the striking thing about England after 1588 was not its exhaustion but its inexhaustible energy, its buoyancy, and its boundless confidence. The explanation of "golden ages" has ever been the despair of historians, and the Age of Shakespeare is no exception. Among the contributing factors, one can point to the steadily expanding population and economy, for which the long peace before 1585 was largely responsible. One can describe the virtues of the Tudor popular despotism which Elizabeth brought to perfection and the broad-based religious settlement which she made. One can point to the long, slow development of English national consciousness, fanned into a sudden blaze of self-confident awareness in the glorious defeat of the Spanish Armada. But in the long run the poetry and drama of the turn of the century, the music and the style of living, the visions of overseas empire and the sense of destiny, everything that we associate with the Elizabethan Age is inexplicable in any simple historical terms.

It is tempting to compare England and Spain, the Protestant and Catholic champions and the two strongest powers in Europe in 1588, at the moment when they grappled with each other. Both were on the periphery of that Europe described at the beginning of this essay. Each had an independence of action which came from having little or no land frontier of its own to defend. Spain was supreme on land, England was soon to be supreme on the seas. Spain produced one of the two colossal literary figures of the turn of the century, Cervantes, and England produced the other, Shakespeare. England like Spain had also developed a sense of her national destiny. It was best expressed by Richard Hakluyt, the preacher, propagandist, and geographer who by narrating the "principal navigations" of the explorers had so much to do with impressing the voyages of discovery upon the imagination of his countrymen and firing them to dreams of colonization and empire overseas. To Hakluyt it was England's destiny to stem the tide of Spanish Catholicism and to build a Protestant counterweight to the Spanish empire in the New World. In a revealing phrase he once prophesied that Englishmen would carry even as far as Japan and the Far East "the incomparable treasure of the trueth of Christianity, and of the Gospell, while we use and exercise common trade with their marchants." A mission to spread the benefits of Protestant Christianity, along with English freedom and the material benefits of advanced industry and trade—this vision was already in evidence before the great queen's death in 1603 in writers like Hakluyt and Protestant buccaneering gentry like Drake. Coming later than the Spanish sense of destiny, it was fashioned partly in conscious opposition to the Spanish dream itself. It looked forward rather than backward, on toward the expanding economy and competitive tendencies of the modern world rather than back to the ordered and organic society of the Middle Ages. But in both dreams there was that peculiar combination of religion and politics, of idealism and materialism, which is the mark of the sixteenth century. Protestant England confronting Catholic Spain, each assured that in its own national interest there lay a religious destiny, this is the typical outcome of the political developments and the religious upheavals of the sixteenth century.

The Mind of the Sixteenth Century

From one point of view, the mind of the sixteenth century, the way men thought and felt, was very remote from our own. It was still a profoundly religious age, in spite of obvious trends toward secularism or the dominance of this-worldly ends and motives. Men accepted the existence of God as readily as we accept the existence of the atom. In the crises of individual and social life, they turned to the resources of religion as naturally and normally as many of us turn to science and social action.

It is no coincidence that the great thinkers of the first half of the century were primarily concerned, almost without exception, with religious problems. But this was a learned concern, a concern of scholars, teachers, and intellectuals, not merely of mystics, prophets, and unlettered people. There probably never was another half-century in European history when Christian scholars had so much influence on so many people. The enthusiasm for what sheer learning could accomplish in this world was communicated by the Humanists to the religious reformers, who wrote not only in Latin but also in the common tongues and whose works were spread by the printing press. Erasmus made his living by research, editing, and writing. Thomas More was a lawyer by profession, but a Christian scholar at heart. Cardinal Ximenes in Spain, John Colet in England, and Lefèvre d'Etaples in France were three of a whole company who left their mark on Biblical scholarship. Luther was a professor of Bible, and one of his biographers calls him a "Biblical Humanist." Calvin always thought of himself as a scholar torn from his beloved books by the call of duty. The religious upheaval was above all an upheaval in thought as well as in experience and emotion. Except for harbingers of a more secular age like Machiavelli, for whom the spiritual world simply did not exist, and Rabelais, whose zest for this world in all its confusion was insatiable, the profoundest minds of the first half of the sixteenth century were concerned with religious problems.

What we call the scientific attitude was evident in only a handful of mathematicians and students of nature who were slowly fitting together experimental technique and mathematical analysis to form what would later be called the scientific method. The two greatest scientific works of the century appeared in the same "wonder year" 1543: Copernicus' *On the Revolutions of the Heavenly Orbs,* which suggested that it was simpler mathematically to assume that the sun, rather than the earth, is the center of the visible universe; and Vesalius' *On the Structure of the Human Body*, the first work on human anatomy since the time of the Greeks to be based upon careful firsthand observation and dissection. Together they represented the two major aspects of science, the theoretical and the experimental. When these two complementary aspects were brought together in the next century by Galileo and Newton, modern science could be said to have come of age. But the sixteenth century witnessed only its adolescence.

From another point of view, the sixteenth century mind was strangely like our own in spite of the differences suggested. It was a time of rapid and bewildering social change. Three centuries before, the thinkers of the high Middle Ages had come to the general conclusion, with Thomas Aquinas and Dante, that in spite of all the surface conflicts the world was ultimately a rational, intelligible, and orderly place—planned, created, and someday to be redeemed by God in Christ. "The Author of the universe is Intelligence," Aquinas had written, echoing Aristotle. It was much harder to believe this in the age of Machiavelli and Luther, Henry VIII and Suleiman the Magnificent, John Calvin and Ignatius of Loyola. If the Christian God was still in control—and only a few yet doubted it—He appeared to be a more majestic and mysterious God than the thirteenth century had imagined, a beleaguered God actively confronting evil, a God in whom will and power were more evident than reason and law. To a very few like Machiavelli it even appeared that God had retired altogether and that man was on his own in this world, compelled to rely on his own shrewdness and force of will to bring some order out of apparent chaos and ceaseless change. It was a time of half-understood change when old ideas and institutions were rapidly losing their meaning and no acceptable substitutes were yet in sight. It was therefore natural that men turned from confidence in the rationality of the universe to faith in will and power and creativity, whether those of God or of man.

Machiavelli glorified the man of *virtù*, the man of virility and virtuosity, freed from older prejudices as to "what ought to be." Luther and Calvin were equally concerned to free God from all the trammels by which men had tried to bind Him in the recent past, for instance, the assumption that He must grant His grace only through the Roman Church and its sacraments. If the four dominating figures in early sixteenth-century statecraft were Charles V, Francis I, Henry VIII, and Suleiman the Magnificent, those of the latter part of the century were Philip II, Elizabeth, Henry of Navarre, and William of Orange. All were persons of great force of will. But it is interesting to note that of the later group all, excepting Philip, were weak at the beginning, and had to combine what Machiavelli called the cunning of the fox with the strength of the lion in order to establish their power. The going was harder for the statesmen of the latter half of the century. The inner spirit of the sixteenth century is revealed in its various facets in Machiavelli's *The Prince;* in the brooding, superhuman, hampered figures of Michelangelo's sculpture; in the startlingly earthy and determined faces which look at us from the canvases of Holbein, that most objective of painters; in the majestic sovereignty both of Calvin's God and of Bodin's ruler; in the iron will of the Jesuit, which could discipline the imagination and subject itself without reserve to the will of a superior. Reason was not forgotten in the sixteenth century, but the age was above all an age of will.

The religious schism appeared at the moment in European history when a strong trend toward political centralization was already under way in many parts of the continent. In some nations such as England, Scotland, and Sweden, Protestantism and national sentiment reinforced each other and political unification was furthered. In the same way Catholicism reinforced patriotism in Spain and Ireland. But in Germany, France, Switzerland, the Netherlands, and Poland—in central Europe generally—religious conflict had a politically disintegrating effect which was more or less serious depending upon the previous history of each country. Like the Communist of the twentieth century, the devoted Calvinist or Jesuit of the sixteenth was swayed by a supranational loyalty which could lead straight to what was called "treason." Religion could enforce patriotism, but it could also undermine it. As communism today is the criterion of patriotism in Russia and the mask of treason in the United States, so to be a Jesuit in Ireland four centuries ago was to be a patriot, to be a Jesuit in England was to be a traitor.

Small wonder that in such a divided age as this men searched desperately for some persuasive principle of authority, visible or invisible. The zealous Roman Catholic found it in the visible church headed by the vicar of Christ, its dogma defined by the Council of Trent. Most Protestants found it in the self-explanatory and self-authenticating Word of God enshrined in the Bible. Some few found it in mystical experience of the divine; still fewer, in the light of human reason applied to all the confusing data of experience. But it became evident to some after mid-century that the root of the trouble was this very search for absolute authority, which inevitably resulted in the bloody clash of absolute and exclusive beliefs. Perhaps truth is not in some formula but in a feeling, said some mystics. Perhaps truth is not so easily defined as some dogmatists think, said the Humanists. Perhaps truth in any ultimate sense is unattainable by human beings, said a few skeptics. "I generally observe," Montaigne wrote drily, "that when a matter is set before them, men are more ready to waste their time in seeking the reason of it than in seeking the truth of it. . . . So much uncertainty is there in all things." If the doubters were right, then the civil wars in Germany, France, and the Netherlands, the war of Protestant England against Catholic Spain, the supranational struggle between Calvinists and Jesuits, were all futile and unnecessary conflicts. As increasing numbers turned in disgust from the fury of the theologians, the cult of the divine-right monarch was waiting to receive them. The last word of the sixteenth century apparently lay with the skeptic Montaigne—his motto "What do I know?" and his self-chosen emblem of a pair of evenly balanced scales—and with Elizabeth of England, who accounted it the glory of her reign that she was "mere English," that she had ruled with the loves of her people, and that she had made no windows into men's souls.

Yet this was not really the last word. It is of the essence of understanding the Age of Reformation to remember that it was still too early for the mass of Europeans to accept a worldly skepticism and a faith in the omnicompetence of the state as the logical way out of their intellectual and institutional difficulties. Among other things, the fact that the sixteenth century witnessed the climax of the witchcraft mania should remind us that there were profound unresolved tensions in European society, untouched by rational control. Europe was shaken in its ancient faith in the priest, but not yet ready to put all its trust in the king. As confidence in the mediaeval church waned and as men began to wonder confusedly whether the secular state could save them, it is not surprising that fear gnawed at their hearts and that they turned (as they still do) either to cynical indifference or to witch-burning. If one thing can be said of the sixteenth-century mind—in contrast with that of the thirteenth before or the eighteenth after—it is that it was not sure of itself. This is to say that the Age of Reformation was the watershed between the Middle Ages and modern times.

Chronological Summary

Suggestions for Further Reading

THE classic one-volume treatment of the period in English is Preserved Smith, *The Age of the Reformation* (New York, 1920). Harold J. Grimm, *The Reformation Era 1500–1600* (New York, 1954), is a well-balanced survey, abreast of recent scholarship. Hajo Holborn, *A History of Modern Germany: The Reformation* (New York, 1959), places the Lutheran movement in its whole economic and political setting. In the Rise of Modern Europe series, Myron P. Gilmore, *The World of Humanism, 1453–1517* (New York, 1952), touches upon the opening of the period, but the next two volumes covering the remainder of the sixteenth century have yet to appear.

The most successful attempts at a synthesis of the age are in French and German. The two relevant volumes in the Peuples et Civilisations series are particularly good: Henri Hauser and Augustin Renaudet, *Les Débuts de l'âge moderne* [1492–1559] (Paris, 1938), and Henri Hauser, *La Prépondérance espagnole* [1559–1660] (Paris, 1933). Gerhard Ritter, *Die Neugestaltung Europas im 16. Jahrhundert: Die kirchlichen und staatlichen Wandlungen im Zeitalter der Reformation und der Glaubenskämpfe* (Berlin, 1950), is the work of a master scholar and stylist. Paul Joachimsen's classic essay on "Die Reformation" may be found in Volume V of the "Propyläen Weltgeschichte" (*Das Zeitalter der religiösen Umwälzung*, Berlin, 1930) and has recently been published separately in somewhat expanded form (Munich, 1951). Fernand Braudel, *La Méditerranée et le monde méditerranéen à l'époque de Philippe II* (Paris, 1949) is a splendid synthesis of the geographical, economic, and political aspects of the history of the later sixteenth century.

There are two recent brief treatments of the religious upheaval: Roland H. Bainton, *The Reformation of the Sixteenth Century* (Boston, 1952), and George L. Mosse, *The Reformation* (Berkshire series; New York, 1953).

On Erasmus, see J. Huizinga, *Erasmus of Rotterdam* (New York, 1952), or Margaret M. Phillips, *Erasmus and the Northern Renaissance* (New York, 1950).

The best short biography of Luther from the Protestant point of view is Roland H. Bainton, *Here I Stand: A Life of Martin Luther* (Mentor Books, 1955). The best from the Catholic point of view is Hartmann Grisar, *Martin Luther: His Life and Work* (St. Louis, 1935). There is a wealth of interesting background material in E. G. Schwiebert, *Luther and His Times* (St. Louis, 1950).

On Calvin's life, see Williston Walker, *Calvin* (New York, 1906); on his thought, François Wendel, *Calvin: Sources et évolution de sa pensée religieuse* (Paris, 1950). John T. McNeill, *The History and Character of Calvinism* (New York, 1954), is a superb survey.

There is no authoritative recent treatment of the Anabaptists in general, but Roland H. Bainton, *The Travail of Religious Liberty* (Philadelphia, 1951), is a good introduction to several of the leading figures of the "left wing." Norman Cohn, *The Pursuit of the Millennium* (London, 1957), traces apocalypticism from the New Testament through the sixteenth century. Max Weber, *The Protestant Ethic and the Spirit of Capitalism*, ed. Talcott Parsons (London, 1930), is a famous essay, originally published in 1905 and the subject of considerable controversy ever since.

Pierre Janelle, *The Catholic Reformation* (Milwaukee, 1948), is an excellent brief treatment of the subject. Hubert Jedin, *A*

History of the Council of Trent, Vol. I (St. Louis, 1957), is the first volume of what will be a definitive account.

Two brief collections of contemporary source materials are useful: *Great Voices of the Reformation,* ed. Harry Emerson Fosdick (New York, 1952); and Roland H. Bainton, *The Age of the Reformation* (Anvil Books, 1956).

On the history of the leading European nations during the period, see R. Trevor Davies, *The Golden Age of Spain* (London, 1937); R. B. Merriman, *The Rise of the Spanish Empire in the Old World and the New,* Vols. III and IV (New York, 1925–1934); Louis Batiffol, *The Century of the Renaissance* [France] (London, 1916); Pieter Geyl, *The Revolt of the Netherlands, 1555–1609* (London, 1932); C. V. Wedgwood, *William the Silent: William of Nassau, Prince of Orange* (New Haven, 1944); S. T. Bindoff, *Tudor England* (Penguin Books, 1950); and G. R. Elton, *England under the Tudors* (London, 1955).

The history of political theory is well covered in J. W. Allen, *A History of Political Thought in the Sixteenth Century* (New York, 1928), and Pierre Mesnard, *L'Essor de la philosophie politique au xvi siècle* (Paris, 1936). Garrett Mattingly, *Renaissance Diplomacy* (London, 1955), is a brilliant account of the development of diplomatic institutions from 1400 to 1600.

Herbert Butterfield, *The Origins of Modern Science, 1300–1800* (London, 1949), is a thoughtful introduction to the subject. A. R. Hall, *The Scientific Revolution 1500–1800* (London, 1954), is more difficult but more penetrating.

Index

Yeoman.